The U.S. Constitution

A Primary Source Investigation
into the Fundamental Law
of the United States

Heather Moehn

Great American Political Documents

The U.S. Constitution

A Primary Source Investigation
into the Fundamental Law
of the United States

Heather Moehn

ROSEN
PRIMARY SOURCE

To my parents, Patrick and Carlene Moehn and
Ken and Nancy Mirman

Published in 2003 by The Rosen Publishing Group, Inc.
29 East 21st Street, New York, NY 10010

Copyright © 2003 by The Rosen Publishing Group, Inc.

First Edition

Library of Congress Cataloging-in-Publication Data

Moehn, Heather.
The U.S. Constitution : a primary source investigation into the fundamental law of the United States/Heather Moehn—1st ed.
  p. cm.—(Great American political documents)
Summary: A historical review of the people, issues, and events that led to the drafting and ratification of the United States Constitution.
Includes bibliographical references and index.
ISBN 0-8239-3804-2 (library binding)
1. Constitutional history—United States—Juvenile literature.
2. United States—Politics and government—1783–1789—
Juvenile literature. [1. Constitutional history—United States.
2. United States—Politics and government—1783–1789.]
I. Title: US Constitution. II. Title. III. Series.
KF4520.Z9 M64 2003
342.73'029—dc21
                                                          2002011223

Manufactured in the United States of America

Cover illustration: *The Signing of the Constitution* by Howard Chandler Christy. Washington stands at the right, and Hamilton, Franklin, and Madison are seated in the center.

Contents

This illustration from an early American woodcut celebrates the framework of laws and freedoms created by the Constitution.

Introduction

> We the People of the United States, in Order to form a more perfect Union, establish Justice, insure domestic Tranquility, provide for the common defence, promote the general Welfare, and secure the Blessings of Liberty to ourselves and our Posterity, do ordain and establish this Constitution for the United States of America.
>
> —Preamble, U.S. Constitution

The role of a government in the lives of its people is a subject that is discussed daily by American citizens and their politicians. More than 200 years ago, similar discussions about the same issues took place among the American colonists. The document that the Founding Fathers developed in response to these concerns—the U.S. Constitution—still tells Americans how their government should function.

The Founding Fathers created the Constitution to deal not only with the political problems they faced but with those of future generations as well. They knew they could not foresee every issue that would arise as the American nation grew, so they created a flexible system of government that was subject to amendment and change. However, they also wanted

to ensure the stability of the government. The amendment process that they devised has worked beautifully to strike a balance between these two needs. The original document remains the nation's political foundation, while the twenty-seven amendments that have been added reflect changes in American society and address issues such as slavery, prohibition, and suffrage.

The term "constitution" means "the principles, institutions, laws, practices, and traditions by which a people carry on their political and governmental life."[1] The United States was the first country to outline those principles and rules in one written document. George Washington called the Constitution "little short of a miracle." Thomas Jefferson called it "the result of the collected wisdom of our country."[2] It has been so successful that it is copied by fledgling democracies around the world.

In discussions about the Constitution, people interpret and reinterpret it daily. To do so, it is necessary to know the thinking behind its various sections and articles. This book tells the story of the drafting and acceptance of the Constitution. It describes the American political experience up to 1787 and explains the events that led to the Constitutional Convention. It reveals the philosophical ideas behind the document and talks about the main issues and the debates that inspired its final form. It describes how the three branches of government developed and how a system of checks and balances was put in place to prevent the concentration of political power. It describes the ratification process and how the Constitution became the supreme law of the land.

In 1792, James Madison wrote, "The people who are the authors of this blessing must also be its guardians. Their eyes must be ever ready to mark, their voices to pronounce, and their arms to repel or repair aggressions on the authority of their Constitution."[3] This statement carries just as much weight today as it did then. It is the responsibility of all Americans to be informed about their rights and the role of government, and to safeguard the U.S. Constitution.

Chapter One

American Constitutional Experience Prior to 1787

Every Bill which shall have passed the House of Representatives and the Senate, shall, before it become a Law, be presented to the President of the United States; If he approve he shall sign it, but if not he shall return it, with his Objections to that House in which it shall have originated, who shall enter the Objections at large on their Journal, and proceed to reconsider it. If after such Reconsideration two thirds of that House shall agree to pass the Bill, it shall be sent, together with the Objections, to the other House, by which it shall likewise be reconsidered, and if approved by two thirds of that House, it shall become a Law. But in all such Cases the Votes of both Houses shall be determined by yeas and Nays, and the Names of the Persons voting for and against the Bill shall be entered on the Journal of each House respectively. If any Bill shall not be returned by the President within ten Days (Sundays excepted) after it shall have been presented to him, the Same shall be a Law, in like Manner as if he had signed it, unless the Congress by their Adjournment prevent its Return, in which Case it shall not be a Law.

—Article 1, Section 7, Clause 2,
U.S. Constitution

Before Americans had the Constitution, they relied on an array of charters, compacts, and royal grants, as well as various British documents, such as the Magna Carta, the Petition of Rights, and the Bill of Rights of 1689,

Many of the basic ideas in our Constitution that limit the power of the government go back as far as the Magna Carta, the "great charter" signed by King John of England in 1215 limiting his absolute power and granting rights to his barons.

to assure them of their rights and privileges as British citizens in America.

As a result, a system of government developed in which power was divided between the British government and the colonial legislatures. The British king and Parliament governed on issues affecting the empire, such as trade, foreign affairs, and defense. The colonial legislatures dealt with local issues, such as transportation, property, and taxation. This system benefited both sides. The British profited from the resources of the colonies

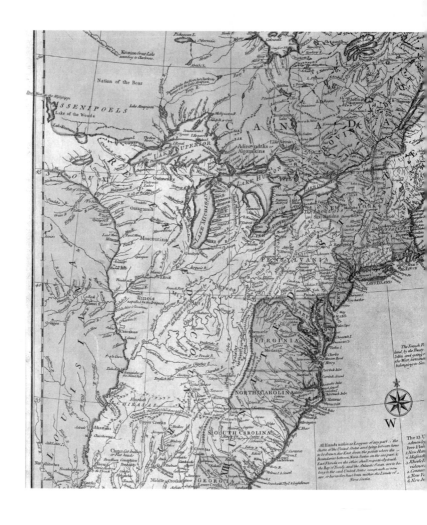

without having to oversee every little detail of administration. The colonies benefited from the protection of the mother country while being free to rule themselves on domestic matters.

The British, however, did not consider their relationship with the colonies to be one of equality. They

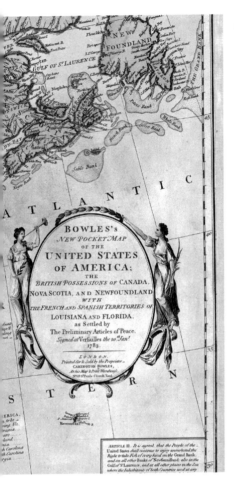

A map of North America showing the thirteen new states of the United States, as settled by the Treaty of Paris in 1783. The British still possessed the territories of Canada, Nova Scotia, and Newfoundland to the north, and the French and Spanish still controlled Louisiana and Florida, respectively, to the south.

believed that all the power resided in the king and Parliament and that the colonial legislatures were completely subordinate to them. In their view, the colonists enjoyed certain freedoms because Parliament chose to allow them. This belief angered the colonists, who viewed America as a self-governing nation of the British Commonwealth. But they didn't challenge British assumptions until 1763. In that year, the events that led to the Revolutionary War unfolded. The result was the dramatic move to a radical new government.

The Road to Revolution

From 1758 to 1763, American colonists fought side-by-side with the British on American soil in the French and Indian War, also known as the Seven Years' War. At the war's conclusion, Britain gained Canada and the land east of the Mississippi River from the French, and Spain held Florida. The price of victory was high, however. Britain's national debt rose from £75,000,000 to £140,000,000 and the country needed to maintain a large army to defend the new land, at an annual cost of £300,000.

The British felt that the colonists should share the cost of this war. Up to this point, the colonists paid few taxes to Britain, and the British began to resent the economic burden of the colonies. To raise money, Parliament began levying new taxes on the colonists, such as the Sugar Act (1764), the Stamp Act (1764), the Townshend Acts (1767), and the Tea Act (1773). Members of Parliament believed

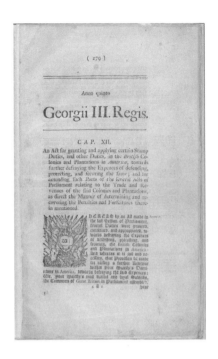

The Stamp Act, which took effect on November 1, 1765, imposed taxes on all documents printed in the American colonies. The act required that a special stamp be put on each document, as shown at the right. The Stamp Act was part of a British effort to raise money to pay for the French and Indian War, but it enraged the American colonists.

that they had the right to tax the colonists through the doctrine of virtual representation. According to this doctrine, a member of Parliament represented the entire empire and not just his geographical region. Thus, the colonies were "virtually" represented by members of Parliament even though no colonists participated.

15

The colonists, however, believed that their interests were so distinct from the English that no British person was capable of representing them. Since they had no representation, they felt that the new taxes violated their rights, and they accused King George III of tyranny. "No taxation without representation!" became the battle cry. American resentment and anger grew, and demonstrations, protests, and riots ensued. Colonists boycotted British goods or destroyed them, as they did at the Boston Tea Party,

A portrait of King George III. Below is a portion of the proclamation he issued in 1775 ordering the suppression of the American rebellion.

Americans throwing the Cargoes of the Tea Ships into the River, at Boston

As shown in this engraving, American colonists dressed as Native Americans threw British tea into Boston Harbor to protest British attempts to monopolize the tea trade. The act became known as the Boston Tea Party and caused the British to close the port of Boston.

where tea from three British ships was dumped into Boston Harbor. Britain responded by passing a series of even more repressive laws, which the colonists called the Intolerable Acts.

The furor over these taxes and Intolerable Acts became so strong that delegates from twelve colonies held a meeting, called the First Continental Congress, on September 5, 1774, to discuss British policies. The congress angrily declared that Parliament's taxes were a violation of "immutable laws of nature, the principles of the English constitution, and the several [colonial] charters or compacts." John Adams stated that Americans were now "degraded below the rank of an Englishman" by laws that constituted "a repeal of Magna Carta."[1]

In April 1775, British soldiers set out to arrest Sam Adams and John Hancock for treason. Paul Revere's famous warning that "the British are coming" helped the men to escape. When the British couldn't find Adams and Hancock, they marched to Lexington, where they encountered armed minutemen, the local militia. The British ordered them to disperse. The colonists started to leave, but they refused to surrender their weapons. Then one of the British soldiers fired the "shot heard 'round the world," and the fight for American independence began.

More than 400 pamphlets written in 1775 and 1776 helped to fuel the colonists' anger. Most illustrated the injustice of British policies. One of the most influential pamphlets was Thomas Paine's *Common Sense*, published in January 1776. In it, he pointed out how ridiculous it was for a huge continent to be ruled by a tiny island. He listed all the reasons America should be independent and proclaimed, "The sun never shined on a cause of greater worth."[2]

On June 7, 1776, the Continental Congress began to write the Declaration of Independence to

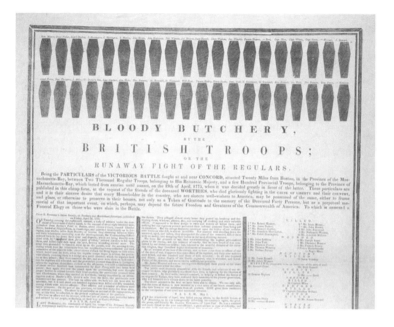

Above is an inflammatory broadside, "Bloody Butchery of the British Troops," that used pictures of coffins to commemorate the forty Americans killed in the fighting at Lexington and Concord. The British suffered sixty-five dead. Below is an engraving of Thomas Paine and the title page of his pamphlet *Common Sense*, an attack on the divine right of kings to rule.

justify its actions. This document stated that King George III had threatened the American people's rights to life, liberty, and the pursuit of happiness. Because the new taxes and policies were tyrannical, the colonists had no choice but to fight.

When the Declaration of Independence was signed on July 4, 1776, the thirteen colonies became thirteen independent nations. They wrote their own constitutions, which declared their sovereignty and outlined the limits of the state governments. There was no national government.

As the Revolutionary War raged on, it became clear that the British would triumph unless the states joined forces. A central authority was needed to oversee the military struggle. Despite the urgent need, reaching an agreement was a long process. It took four years to debate and discuss the various issues. The resulting plan, detailed in a document formally called the Articles of Confederation and Perpetual Union, became effective on March 1, 1781.

The Articles of Confederation

Under the Articles of Confederation, states retained their "sovereignty, freedom, and independence"[3] and entered into "a firm league of friendship with each other."[4] The central government existed only to aid cooperation among the states. It had no real power because the colonists feared that a strong national government could become just as tyrannical as the one they were fighting.

In the confederation government, a one-house Congress consisted of delegates chosen by the states. They were not required to attend meetings, and often so few did that business could not be completed. Although a president of Congress was elected, he was merely a figurehead and had no real authority. When Congress was able to pass laws, they were meaningless because Congress lacked the authority to make the states obey. Each state had a single vote in Congress, and any change to the Articles of Confederation had to be agreed upon unanimously.

The problems with the Articles of Confederation became apparent soon after the document was accepted. Because Congress could not enforce laws, it could not collect taxes and states gave whatever they wanted—usually amounts far below what had been requested. The national government was so financially unstable that when a messenger brought news of British general Cornwallis's defeat and surrender at Yorktown, there was not enough money in the treasury to pay

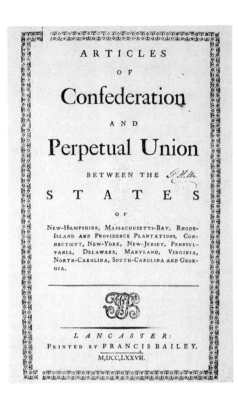

At left is the first printing of the Articles of Confederation. At bottom right is John Dickinson, who was principally responsible for drafting the Articles. At top right is a portrait of Roger Sherman, who signed the Declaration of Independence, the Articles of Confederation, and the Constitution.

the messenger. Each member of Congress had to donate a dollar from his own pocket.

The states also ignored congressional requests during the war for supplies, clothing, wagons, and troops (unless the fighting was on their soil). As the commander of the Continental army, George Washington felt that the national government was nothing more than a "rope of sand." He remarked that "the Confederation appears to me to be a shadow without substance."[5]

Despite its weaknesses, the Articles of Confederation gave the states enough strength to win the Revolutionary War and to negotiate the Treaty of Paris in 1783. No other colony had successfully broken with a European power before this time. Americans felt they were destined to become the greatest nation in the world. However, before America could reach its full potential, it had to survive the critical period following the war. "The American war is over," wrote Benjamin Rush, a Philadelphia statesman, "but that is far from being the case with the American Revolution. On the contrary, nothing but the first act of the great drama is closed."[6] The second act opened when the "firm league of friendship" of the confederation fell apart. Now that the immediate danger of war had passed, the states paid even less attention to Congress and more to their own issues. They began quarreling with each other about tariffs, commerce, and land.

Debt caused by the war added to the country's problems. America's credit plunged overseas, making it difficult for the new nation to be taken seriously by European powers. Economic problems at home also plagued the states. Inflation was staggering—in some areas one pound of tea cost more than $100. Families struggled to make ends meet and begged their legislators for relief. Some states suspended the collection of taxes and debts and allowed debtors to disregard the terms of loans. Others began printing paper money that was not backed by gold or silver. This allowed debtors to pay creditors with money that was worth far less than the original amount loaned. The United States was in critical condition. Something had to be done, George Washington wrote a friend, "to avert the humiliating and contemptible figure we are about to make on the annals of mankind."[7]

Since the end of the Revolutionary War, Maryland and Virginia had been fighting over rights to the Potomac River and Chesapeake Bay. Washington believed the issue was hindering expansion into the western territories and suggested holding a conference at his Mount Vernon home to resolve the issue. Delegates from the two states met for three days in March 1785. The men settled their differences and even made additional agreements. Their success inspired them to schedule a meeting of all the states in Annapolis, Maryland, to discuss expanding Congress's role in national commerce.

The Annapolis Convention was a disappointment. Only five states sent delegates. The others feared losing local power and stayed home. With such a small turnout, the organizers' goals could not be accomplished. However, they decided to use the meeting to advance their views about strengthening the national government. Alexander Hamilton, a delegate from New York, wrote a report requesting that the states send delegates to another convention in Philadelphia to discuss amending the Articles of Confederation to give the national government enough power to respond to the growing needs of the country. Sending the report was a bold move. Changes to the Articles of Confederation required the unanimous approval of all states. Eight states had already refused to discuss expanding Congress's role in commerce. Why would they agree to further changes to the Articles of Confederation?

Shays's Rebellion

A violent uprising in Massachusetts moved the reluctant states to action. Citizens in Massachusetts were burdened with heavy debt and a poor economy, as were citizens in other states. Massachusetts, however, refused to print paper money or change the terms of loans. This had a devastating effect on farmers, many of whom were thrown in jail and had their farms confiscated.

This wood engraving is the only known image of Daniel Shays, pictured on the left. In 1786 in Springfield, Massachusetts, Shays led a rebellion of indebted farmers protesting high taxes. The difficulties in raising troops to suppress the rebellion convinced many Americans that a stronger government was needed.

A group of farmers led by Captain Daniel Shays attacked courthouses to stop foreclosures and threatened to take over the national arsenal in Springfield. Because Massachusetts had not wanted to pay for an army after the Revolution, the state was helpless. The national government also lacked the resources to help. Finally, wealthy families donated enough money to hire new troops and the rebellion was stopped. News of the revolt spread quickly and terrified the leaders of the other states. They worried that similar uprisings might happen within their borders. Anarchy seemed a real threat, and the national government was too weak to stop it. Thus, when the states' leaders received Hamilton's report, they quickly appointed delegates and made preparations to attend. Congress gave its permission for the delegates to meet "for the sole and express purpose of revising the Articles of Confederation."[8]

The Delegates

In total, fifty-five delegates from twelve states (Rhode Island refused to send delegates) attended the convention at various times. All the men were knowledgeable and experienced in government. Many had contributed to the drafting of the Articles of Confederation and the Declaration of Independence. The majority had served in the Confederation Congress and some were governors or former governors. Others had fought for America's freedom in the Revolutionary War. At a time when higher education was rare, almost half the delegates had degrees. The group included lawyers, merchants, doctors, planters, and politicians. The delegates were such a distinguished group of Americans that Thomas Jefferson, who was serving as ambassador to France, called the convention "an assembly of demigods."[9]

Although there were many similarities among the delegates—all were white, male property owners who were mostly Protestant—they came to the convention with a wide variety of goals and motives. The commercial interests of the northern merchants differed greatly from the concerns of the plantation owners in the South. The delegates from small states feared domination by the large and more populous states. And the issue of slavery overshadowed every discussion about the future of the United States. Regardless of their differences, the delegates knew they had an important task. America needed a stronger government to recover from war and to become a powerful nation. The delegates realized that the Philadelphia Convention might be their only chance to make the experiment in independence a success.

Chapter Two

The Philadelphia Convention

Clause 1:

The executive Power shall be vested in a President of the United States of America. He shall hold his Office during the Term of four Years, and, together with the Vice President, chosen for the same Term, be elected, as follows:

Clause 2:

Each State shall appoint, in such Manner as the Legislature thereof may direct, a Number of Electors, equal to the whole Number of Senators and Representatives to which the State may be entitled in the Congress: but no Senator or representative, or Person holding an Office of Trust or Profit under the United States, shall be appointed an Elector.

Clause 3:

The Electors shall meet in their respective States, and vote by Ballot for two Persons, of whom one at least shall not be an Inhabitant of the same State with themselves. And they shall make a List of all the Persons voted for, and of the Number of Votes for each; which List they shall sign and certify, and transmit sealed to the Seat of the Government of the United States, directed to the President of the Senate. The President of the Senate shall, in the Presence of the Senate and House of Representatives, open all the Certificates, and the Votes shall then be counted. The Person having the greatest Number of Votes shall be the President, if such Number be a Majority of the whole Number of Electors appointed; and if there be more than one who have such Majority, and have an equal Number of Votes, then the House of Representatives shall immediately chuse by Ballot one of them for President; and if no Person have a Majority, then from the five highest on the List the said House shall in like Manner chuse the President. But in chusing the President, the Votes shall be taken by States, the Representation from each State having one Vote; A quorum for this Purpose shall consist of a Member or Members from two thirds of the States, and a Majority of all the States shall be necessary to a Choice. In every Case, after the Choice of the President, the Person having the greatest Number of Votes of the Electors shall be the Vice President. But if there should remain two or more who have equal Votes, the Senate shall chuse from them by Ballot the Vice President.

—Article II, Section 1, U.S. Constitution

James Madison was one of the "demigods" of the Philadelphia Convention. In fact, he is known as the father of the Constitution. He helped to organize both the Mount Vernon Conference and the Annapolis Convention, and worked tirelessly to promote the Philadelphia Convention. He believed that only a strong national government could save the United States

Pictured at top, George Washington addresses the delegates at the Constitutional Convention in 1787. Below left is a portrait of James Madison. Below right is a page of the voluminous notes Madison took at the convention of other delegates' speeches. This page describes the election of Washington as chairman of the convention on the first day.

Λ

from ruin, and he planned to develop such a government at the convention.

Madison would have a hard time being a politician today, when appearances and charisma are so important. He was a small man. Someone once said he was "no bigger than half a piece of soap."[14] He was also shy and quiet, especially in large crowds, but he made up for his timidity by always being thoroughly prepared and organized. His contemporaries had enormous respect for him. William Pierce of Georgia wrote, "He blends together the profound politician with the scholar . . . From a spirit of industry and application which he possesses in a most eminent degree, he always comes forward the best informed man of any point in debate."[1]

To prepare for the convention, Madison spent months studying the political systems of ancient and modern civilizations. He read hundreds of books: encyclopedias, histories, biographies, memoirs, and works on political theory, as well as books by philosophers and men of the Enlightenment. He wanted to know which governments worked and, more important, which failed. Madison compared these various governments in a paper called "Notes on Ancient and Modern Confederacies." He then looked specifically at America and wrote a second paper, "Vices of the Political System of the United States," outlining the weaknesses of the confederacy.[2] By the time he arrived in Philadelphia, Madison had concrete ideas about how to strengthen the American government.

Philosophical Foundations

The theories of John Locke, a seventeenth-century English philosopher, strongly influenced the colonists during the Revolution. Locke claimed that power resides in the people, not the government. People decide to give allegiance to a government and its laws in order to protect their natural rights to life, liberty, and property. When a government fails to secure those rights, the people have an obligation to replace it.

Madison agreed that the power of government is derived from the people, but he also understood that people divide into groups that try to gain power over other people. In his "Vices" paper, Madison wrote, "All civilized societies are divided into different interests and factions, as they happen to be creditors or debtors, rich or poor, husbandmen [farmers], merchants, or manufacturers, members of different religious sects, followers of different political leaders, inhabitants of different districts, owners of different

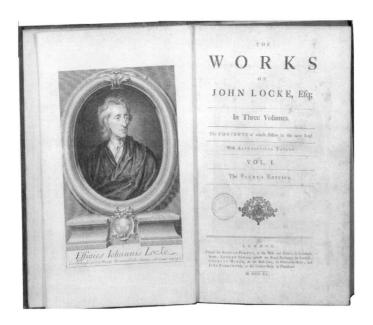

The Works of John Locke. Locke was a liberal English political philosopher who argued that governments derive their power from the people and govern only with their consent. When that consent is withdrawn, Locke argued, a government become illegitimate.

kinds of property, etc., etc."³ From his studies, Madison learned that when governments were unable to balance these different interests and factions, there were disastrous results. He concluded that the American government needed to accept the existence of factions and try to keep them balanced so one group would not be able to control or usurp the rights of another. How to do so was a tough question.

In a republican government, power is held by the citizens who vote and is exercised by the elected

officials who govern according to law. People tradi-
tionally believed that only small, homogeneous
societies could sustain republican governments.
However, by the time of Madison's studies, the
Scottish philosopher David Hume had argued that
larger republics could be successful because factions
would have a harder time joining together into
majorities that could tyrannize the minorities.
Madison saw this swallowing up of factions in a
larger republic as the solution to the crisis in
America. He explained why in the "Vices" paper:
"The society becomes broken into a greater variety
of interests and pursuits of passions, which check
each other, whilst those who may feel a common
sentiment have less opportunity of communication
and concert."[4]

The work of the French writer Charles de
Montesquieu gave Madison an idea of how to divide
power in the government. Montesquieu believed that
governmental powers needed to be separated and balanced to guarantee individual rights and freedoms.
The best way, he determined, was to form separate
executive, legislative, and judicial branches. By the
time he arrived in Philadelphia for the Constitutional
Convention, Madison had formed several convictions
as a result of his intensive studies. First, the Articles of

Confederation needed to be replaced, not revised. Second, a strong central authority was needed to guide the country. And the new government itself had to divide its powers to avoid tyranny.

Terrible rainstorms occurred the week before the convention, making the roads to Philadelphia muddy and dangerous. Nevertheless, Madison arrived eleven days early and urged his fellow Virginia delegates to get there as quickly as possible. On the planned opening

The Assembly Room in Independence Hall in Philadelphia, the site of the signing of the Constitution in 1787. Here Washington presided over the debate on the new form of government and became its first president.

day of the convention, May 14, 1787, only the delegates from Virginia and Pennsylvania were present. The start of the convention had to be postponed. Madison took advantage of the extra time to refine his ideas further. He knew that the first group to present a plan would set the agenda for the convention, and he wanted his ideas to lead. The Virginians met every day in the Indian Queen Tavern and created a blueprint for the new government, which became known as the Virginia Plan.[5]

On May 25, 1787, enough states were represented to begin the convention. As the delegates made their way to the red brick State House, now called Independence Hall, an aura of great excitement surrounded them. A Philadelphia newspaper had written, "The political existence of the United States perhaps depends on the result of the Convention."[6] Another added, "All the fortunes of the future are involved in this momentous undertaking."[7] The delegates met in the East Room of the State House, a large room with a high plaster ceiling. Wide windows were located on two sides with wooden blinds to block the sun. The far wall was paneled and painted gray. The presiding officer sat against this wall in a high-back chair. The delegates shared large tables covered in green cloth. Although the building was well designed, it was not very comfortable. The summer of 1787 was hot and humid, and the room was airless and stifling. When the men opened the windows to try to get a breeze, black flies swarmed in and bit them. Despite the discomfort, the delegates met six days a week from early morning to late afternoon for four long months.

Madison took a seat in the front of the room in order to hear everything that was said. He planned to take comprehensive notes about every discussion and debate in order to leave an accurate record for posterity. Because of these notes, published after his death, Americans know the story of their Constitution.

As the first order of business, the delegates unanimously elected George Washington as the presiding officer. Then the secretary read the credentials of each delegate, and the rules of procedure were defined. One of the rules determined how votes would be taken. Each state got one vote, as in the Continental Congress, and that vote was determined by the majority of individuals within a state delegation. Sometimes the delegates from a state would split their votes, leaving them unable to register an official vote.

Another important rule concerned the recording of how each individual voted in the minutes. It was argued that if votes were noted early in the convention, delegates might feel bound to stand by their

A contemporary engraving of George Washington addressing the Constitutional Convention in 1787. He was already a war hero and the most respected statesman in the country.

earlier opinions and would not be willing to compromise. To give them freedom to change their minds on issues, it was decided not to record the votes of individuals, but only the states.

The most controversial rule, and one that probably would not be allowed today, was that of secrecy. Supporters of this rule were worried about the effect of public opinion on the proceedings. Delegates were forbidden from speaking about the convention with anyone, and sentries were placed at the doors and windows to stop eavesdroppers.

A portrait of Edmund Jennings Randolph, the first attorney general of the United States. An eloquent speaker, he argued forcefully for a strong federal government.

Washington took this rule so seriously that he stopped writing about the proceedings in his personal diary.

With these procedures in place, the delegates were ready to get down to business. Washington turned to Edmund Randolph, the thirty-four-year-old governor of Virginia, to present the Virginia Plan. Randolph was a handsome man with strong features and dark loose hair. He was also an eloquent speaker and an excellent choice for introducing the plan. He began by describing the serious problems that the confederacy had been unable to solve. Then he carefully described each part of the Virginia Plan and how it would fix those problems.

The Virginia Plan

The government under the Virginia Plan would have three branches—legislative, executive, and judiciary. The new legislature would be bicameral, meaning that it would have two houses. Representation in both houses was to be based on either population or the amount of money contributed by the states to the central government. These details differed from the Articles of Confederation, which called for a one-house legislature giving all states one vote regardless of size. Members of the lower house were to be elected by the people, and those members were to elect representatives for the upper house from nominations from the state legislatures. Again, this departed from the Articles of Confederation, which allowed states to assign any number of representatives who could be replaced at the state's will.

Congress was to have the same authority as it did under the Articles of Confederation, with the addition of several important powers. It would be able to make laws in cases in which the states were "incompetent" or where state action would inter-rupt "the harmony of the United States."[8] It also could veto any state law that conflicted with a national law, and it gained the power to make a state obey acts of Congress.

The executive, a single president, and the judiciary would be elected by Congress and would have much greater power than under the Articles of Confederation. They would form a council of revision that would have the authority to veto acts of Congress. With such a division of power, the Virginia Plan created a system of checks and balances that would keep one branch from dominating the others.

It was late afternoon when Randolph finished his presentation, so the convention adjourned for the day.

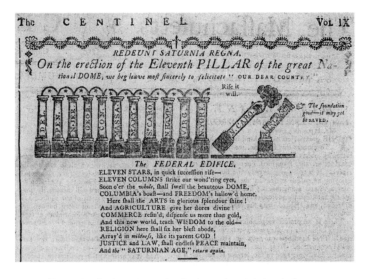

An allegorical drawing depicting the United States as a great dome supported by those states that quickly ratified the Constitution. North Carolina and Rhode Island, which withheld ratification for a time, are depicted here as a threat to the stability of the union.

That night at taverns and boardinghouses across Philadelphia, the delegates no doubt reflected on the Virginia Plan and the monumental task of establishing a strong government. Most delegates agreed with Washington's opinion that the government under the confederacy was nothing more than "a rope of sand." They knew that the national government needed to be a rope strong enough to support the entire nation. Each delegate, however, had different ideas about how this would be best accomplished. They had to figure out a way to weave their disparate ideas into one conception of government.

This was an arduous task. State and regional interests were usually so tangled that it took weeks to work through an issue. Often, when the delegates thought they had solved all their problems and were beginning to come together, another argument was made that caused the whole thing to unravel. They also could not focus on one point at a time. All the issues were so intertwined that a discussion involving one concept would affect something they had already decided. At a few points, many delegates thought they would have to admit defeat and abandon the entire project. But they did not give up.

Chapter Three

The Main Issues

Representatives and direct Taxes shall be apportioned among the several States which may be included within this Union, according to their respective Numbers, which shall be determined by adding to the whole Number of free Persons, including those bound to Service for a Term of Years, and excluding Indians not taxed, three fifths of all other Persons. The actual Enumeration shall be made within three Years after the first Meeting of the Congress of the United States, and within every subsequent Term of ten Years, in such Manner as they shall by Law direct. The Number of Representatives shall not exceed one for every thirty Thousand, but each State shall have at Least one Representative; and until such enumeration shall be made, the State of New Hampshire shall be entitled to chuse three, Massachusetts eight, Rhode-Island and Providence Plantations one, Connecticut five, New-York six, New Jersey four, Pennsylvania eight, Delaware one, Maryland six, Virginia ten, North Carolina five, South Carolina five, and Georgia three.

—Article I, Section 2, Clause 3,
U.S. Constitution

The day after Edmund Randolph presented the Virginia Plan, the Convention turned into a Committee of the Whole to discuss it. The Committee of the Whole was an ancient device used in Britain's House of Commons. When sitting as the committee, the delegates informally debated

issues without making binding decisions. Instead, they developed recommendations to be finalized later in the convention. The committee's discussions lasted from May 30 to June 19, at which time the delegates returned to the convention format. The debates were long, passionate, and divisive. The major disputes were between the Federalists, who favored a strong central government, and the Antifederalists, who feared the tyranny of a strong government. There were other issues between the small and large states, and between the different economic perspectives of the northern and southern states.

Congress had restricted the convention to amending the Articles of Confederation, and many delegates were content with that goal. Others, however, aimed to do much more. The first major debate of the convention was between those who wanted a strong central government and those who wanted the states to retain their authority and independence. While meeting with the other Virginia delegates before the convention started, Randolph wavered between the two sides. He was troubled that Madison wanted to scrap the Articles of Confederation without trying to fix it. To curb the radical Virginia Plan, he suggested a resolution stating that the Articles of

Confederation "be so corrected and enlarged as to accomplish the objects proposed by their institution; namely, common defense, security of liberty, and general welfare."[1] When Madison reluctantly agreed to its inclusion, Randolph showed his appreciation and support by agreeing to read the Virginia Plan to the convention.

Randolph must have struggled with his desire to repair the confederacy and his knowledge that greater changes were necessary. Finally, he agreed to replace his resolution with three new ones suggested by Gouverneur Morris from Philadelphia. The first two stated that neither a confederation of the states nor treaties among them could accomplish what the United States needed. The third boldly declared "that a national government ought to be established consisting of a supreme Legislative, Executive, and Judiciary."[2]

After Randolph read the new resolutions, the delegates stared at him in silence as they grasped the meaning of a supreme national government. Charles Pinckney from South Carolina broke the silence and asked if Randolph meant to abolish the state governments entirely.[3] Handsome, vain, and ambitious, Pinckney desperately wanted to make an impression at the convention and even lied about

A portrait of Gouverneur Morris of Philadelphia, who advocated a strong central government at the Constitutional Convention. Morris was a powerful speaker who argued that a weak national government would eventually succumb to foreign tyranny.

his age so that his accomplishments seemed more remarkable (he said he was twenty-four when he was really twenty-nine). With this question, he voiced the concern of those who feared that a strong national government would absorb and destroy the sovereign states.

Arguments erupted as the delegates struggled, as Randolph did, to establish their positions. Businessmen knew there were advantages to a national government, but they did not want it telling them how to conduct their affairs. Delegates from the most populated southern states saw that large states benefited under the Virginia Plan with proportional representation, but they feared that a strong central government would affect slavery and the markets for their agricultural goods.

Gouverneur Morris tried to calm the delegates by explaining how the strong national government would help the country. Morris was one of the most outspoken delegates at the convention. He was a vivacious man who enjoyed life to the fullest. The loss of his left leg in a carriage accident did not slow him down at all. He paced the room as he spoke, and the thump from his wooden leg punctuated his statements. "A federal government which each party may violate at pleasure cannot answer the purpose," he said. "One government is better calculated to prevent wars or render them less expensive or bloody than many. We had better take a supreme government now than a despot twenty years hence, for come he must."[4]

The Virginian George Mason also spoke. He pointed out that the government in the Virginia Plan operated directly on the people, not the states. A concept of citizenship tied to the states was a major weakness of the Confederate Congress. Roger Sherman of Connecticut agreed that Congress was too limited in the confederacy, but he wasn't ready "to make too great inroads on the existing system."[5] Other delegates also expressed doubts. Charles Coatesworth Pinckney, the younger Pinckney's cousin from South Carolina, and Elbridge Gerry, a merchant from Massachusetts, questioned the right of the convention to annihilate the confederation and overthrow the existing government.[6]

After intense debate, the delegates voted on the issue. The Federalists had provided strong arguments, and the new resolution passed. This was one of the biggest moments of the Constitutional Convention. In deciding to create a supreme national government, the delegates abandoned the Articles of Confederation. Although the vote was not binding and would be challenged again, from that point on the delegates set their sights on devising a new government.

Representation

While the first resolution of the Virginia Plan gave the convention a fiery start, the next one—regarding representation in the legislature—almost ended it. Although other issues were discussed during the next few weeks, the debates always centered on the rights of suffrage and legislative representation.

Under the Articles of Confederation, each state received one vote in the one-house Congress. Madison and the other delegates from the more populous states felt that this system was unfair. It seemed

clear that because Congress represented the people, states with more people should have more votes. The delegates from populous states knew that the less populous states would not like giving up their equal stature in Congress, but they believed that the delegates from those states would see the injustice in the previous arrangement. They were not prepared for

A colored engraving, possibly by the artist Amos Doolittle, depicting the debate in Connecticut over the Constitution between Federalists and Antifederalists. The state is depicted as a wagon sinking in the mud, and the wagon's driver warns, "Gentlemen this Machine is deep in the mire and you are divided as to its releaf." The caption below reads "A House Divided Against Itself Cannot Stand."

the determination of the less populous states to keep their equal representation.

The delegates from the sparsely populated states were also not prepared for the force with which the delegates from the populous states pushed for proportional representation. Because the issue had already been debated during the creation of the Articles of

Confederation, the less populous states felt that it did not need to be discussed again. The "one state–one vote" system was even being used in the Constitutional Convention itself. Furthermore, the less populous states saw that if representation were proportional, the populous states would dominate Congress and leave the less populous states powerless. How could the more populous states expect them to agree to that?

The arguments of the less populous states were explosive. John Dickinson declared that Delaware's delegates would walk out of the convention if the one vote per state principle were changed. William Paterson told the delegates from the more populous states that New Jersey would "rather submit to a monarch, to a despot, than to such a fate."[7] By June 13, every resolution of the Virginia Plan had been debated and voted on in the Committee of the Whole. The delegates switched back to the convention to finalize the details. The representatives from the less populous states were shocked that the Virginia Plan's system of proportional representation had made it this far.

The New Jersey Plan

William Paterson requested that the convention adjourn so he could put together a new plan before a final vote was taken on the Virginia Plan. On June 15, he presented the New Jersey Plan to the convention. Paterson opened his description of the New Jersey Plan by explaining that it was a revision of the Articles of Confederation. He felt that in the Virginia Plan the delegates had gone too far and that the people would reject such widespread change. He stated, "Our object is not such a Government as may be best in itself, but such a one as our constituents have authorized us to prepare and as they will approve."[8] The major difference between the two plans was that the New Jersey Plan called for a one-house legislature with an equal number of members from each state.

James Madison was in no mood to consider the New Jersey Plan, especially after John Dickinson taunted him by saying, "You see the consequence of pushing things too far."[9] He attacked the New Jersey Plan with a masterful speech that displayed the knowledge that he had gained from his earlier studies.

Madison stated that any plan for government needed to "preserve the Union" and "provide a government that will remedy the evils felt by the States."[10] He then dissected the New Jersey Plan and showed how it failed on those accounts. Perhaps the most convincing part of Madison's

The Virginia Plan

A bicameral legislature with the House of Representatives and the Senate

Government acts directly on citizens

Representation in legislature based on population or money contributed to central government

A single executive (president)

The desire of the majority would prevail

National legislature has authority to act when states are incompetent or when states' actions would interrupt the harmony of the union

Executive given the power to veto legislature

National government can be ratified by delegates elected by the people for the purpose of ratification

The New Jersey Plan

A one-house legislature

Government acts on states

Each state given equal representation in legislature

An executive council

A small minority would be able to control (because each state has an equal number of votes)

Congress given additional powers only in a few instances when states act inappropriately

Executive not given power to veto

Changes must be approved by all the state legislatures

speech was his argument regarding what would happen when the vast western territories formed states. He believed that the new states would eventually outnumber the original thirteen. If equal representation existed, the new states would be able to outvote the old ones. On the other hand, if proportional voting existed, the more populated east would be safe from the ideas of the westerners.

On June 19, the delegates voted between the two plans. The Virginia Plan won seven states to three. By the rules of the convention, the Virginia Plan, as modified by the Committee of the Whole, would now be finalized in the convention. But the less populous states still refused to give up equal representation.

Roger Sherman suggested a compromise. Sherman was a remarkable politician, although he is often forgotten by history. He was the only person to sign the Declaration of Independence, the Articles of Confederation, and the Constitution. He did not have the education or wealth of many of the other delegates. He was a farm boy who was self-taught. Despite his humble beginnings, he was an important man in the eighteenth century and highly respected by his peers. Sherman suggested that there be proportional representation in the lower house, and an equal number of votes for each state in the Senate.

Then both the large and small states, in terms of population, would have part of what they wanted. Although this seemed fair, the more populous states believed they could get proportional representation in both houses and refused to consider the idea.

Anger and flaring tempers filled the room with more heat than the Philadelphia summer. The arguments continued without pause. Benjamin Franklin tried to calm the delegates by suggesting that each session begin with a prayer. Even that idea was argued about. Some pointed out that there were no funds to pay a minister, and others worried about what the public would think. Alexander Hamilton was rumored to have proclaimed that the delegates did not need any "foreign aid."[11]

The moment to vote in the convention between equal and proportional representation in the lower house was nearing. The less populous states had one last chance to argue their case. Luther Martin was delegated to give the final presentation. He was one of the best-known and most well-respected lawyers in Maryland at the time. A brilliant man, he was highly regarded for his hard work and skill in arguing court cases. Unfortunately, he also drank a great deal and often created embarrassing situations. At the convention, he often bored the other delegates with his long speeches. William Pierce said, "[He] possesses a good deal of information, but he has a very bad delivery, and so extremely prolix, that he never speaks without tiring the patience of all who hear him."[12] His speech at this crucial time was no different. He went on for two days vehemently arguing that representation should be equal. But his arguments wandered off on tangents and his main points were buried beneath layers of disorganized information.

Some historians think that if Martin's speech had been solidly reasoned, enough states could have been convinced to vote for equal representation. Instead, the vote on June 29 was in favor of proportional representation in the lower house by six states to four. Although the less populous states were beaten in one house, they were determined to win equal representation in the Senate.

Oliver Ellsworth from Connecticut made the first motion that each state receive an equal vote in the Senate. Gunning Bedford from Delaware warned that the more populous states would abuse their power if given proportional representation in both houses. When the delegates from the more populous states insisted they would never injure the less populous states, Bedford cried, "I do not, gentlemen, trust you!"[13]

On July 2, the delegates voted on representation in the Senate. The less populous states threatened to walk out of the convention if they did not get equal representation. This was a critical moment, and all watched tensely as the vote was taken. The vote was split five to five! The convention was deadlocked and in danger of ending. Charles Cotesworth Pinckney stated that although he did not want to abandon proportional representation, some sort of compromise had to be reached. He suggested that a committee be formed with one man from each state to figure out something.[14] The delegates realized that without a compromise, the convention was finished. One by one, every state except Pennsylvania voted to form a committee. The men chosen to serve were the ones known for their ability to find middle ground: Elbridge Gerry, Oliver Ellsworth, Robert Yates, William Paterson, Benjamin Franklin, Gunning Bedford, Luther Martin, George Mason, William Davie, John Rutledge, and Abraham Baldwin.

While the committee members struggled to reach a compromise and save the Constitutional Convention, the other delegates celebrated Independence Day. On July 5, Elbridge Gerry read the committee's report to the convention. It called for proportional representation in the lower house with one member for every 40,000 inhabitants. If a state had fewer than 40,000 people, it would be allowed one representative (later in the convention the number would be lowered to 30,000). In the upper house, each state would be given an equal vote. The report also stated that money bills could only originate in the lower house, and the Senate could not alter or amend them. This was to assure the more populous states that the less populous states would not authorize expenditures that would have to be paid principally by the more populous states.

Although the convention voted to accept the committee's recommendation, no one liked the result. The delegates were extremely discouraged. Washington wrote, "Our councils are now, if possible, in a worse train than ever . . . In a word, I almost despair of seeing a favorable issue to the proceedings of the Convention, and do therefore repent having had any agency in the business."[15] The arguments continued until July 16 when a vote on the compromise was finally taken. It passed five states to four. At this time, the delegates from the more populous states realized they would never get proportional representation in both houses and decided to accept the outcome.

Six of the most important delegates to the Second Constitutional Convention of 1776

North Versus South

While the main conflicts thus far were between the Federalists and Antifederalists, and between states with different size populations, Madison believed another, more important division existed. He asserted, "The states are divided into different interests, not by their difference of size, but by other circumstances, the most material of which result partly from climate but principally from the effects of their having, or not having, slaves. These two causes concur in forming the great division of interests in the United States. It did not lie between the large and small states: It lay between the Northern and Southern."[16] Indeed, the fight between the North and South proved to be one of the fiercest of that summer.

On June 11, the issue of proportional representation was voted on first, but it was not clear whether representatives would be determined on the basis of a state's population or its wealth. James Wilson suggested using population, and in order to gain the support of the southern states, he added that all "free persons" and "three-fifths of all other persons" would be counted.[17] The delegates knew that by "other persons," he meant slaves. The formula for counting three-fifths of slaves had already been proposed in 1783, when Congress had decided how to levy taxes. At the time, the northern states felt that the southern states would be undertaxed unless slaves were counted. By the time of the convention, eleven of the thirteen states had approved this formula for taxation.

Now the delegates argued over whether slaves should be viewed as people or property. Gouverneur Morris asked, "Upon what principle is it that the slaves shall be computed in the representation? Are they men? Then make them citizens and let them vote. Are they property? Why then is no other property included?"[18] Elbridge Gerry added, "Why then should the blacks, who were property in the South, be in the rule of representation more than the cattle and horses of the North?"[19]

Despite the arguments against counting slaves in the population, Wilson's motion passed nine states to two. However, Madison's warning about slavery being the major division between states proved to be prophetic. The issue arose again at the end of the convention as the Committee of Detail was assigned to create the first complete draft of the new Constitution. Before the Committee of Detail met, Charles Coatesworth Pinckney warned the committee members, "[If you] should fail to insert some security to the Southern states against an emancipation of slaves and taxes on exports, I shall be bound by duty to my state to vote against their report."[20] The committee listened to Pinckney and inserted the clause: "No tax or duty shall be laid by the legislature on articles exported from any state; nor on the migration or importation of such persons as the several states shall think proper to admit; nor shall such migration or importation be prohibited."[21]

After two days of debate, the delegates approved the section stating that there were to be no taxes on state exports. However, the section about neither taxing nor prohibiting the slave trade caused more angry discussions. Luther Martin argued against it. "As five slaves are to be counted as three free men in the apportionment of Representatives, such a clause will leave an encouragement to this traffic. Secondly, slaves weaken one part of the Union which the other parts are bound to protect. The privilege of importing them is therefore unreasonable. And thirdly, it is inconsistent with the principles of the revolution and dishonorable to the American character to have such a feature in the Constitution."[22]

Delegates from the southern states argued that the slave trade should not be taken away from them. Charles Pinckney and Abraham Baldwin stated that

Slaves work in the fields as their overseer looks on. The Constitution granted slaves no rights or liberties, but counted them in determining states' tax burdens and representation in Congress.

if left to themselves, the southern states would probably phase out importing slaves anyway. James Wilson immediately challenged them. "If South Carolina and Georgia are themselves disposed to get rid of the importation of slaves," he said, "they will never refuse to unite because the importation might be prohibited."[23] The southern states assured the northern states that they would refuse to accept the Constitution without this clause. The northern states threatened to be equally stubborn about accepting it without a limit on the slave trade. Finally, Gouverneur Morris suggested appointing yet another committee to find a compromise.

Three days later, on August 25, the committee proposed that Congress be forbidden to end the slave trade before the year 1800. It would be able to tax imported slaves, but at a rate no higher than the average of other imported duties. Charles Coatesworth Pinckney moved to extend the period eight years, from 1800 to 1808. The convention adopted the motion seven states to four. With that vote, the last of the major disputes was resolved.

Chapter Four

The Three Branches of Government

Section 1.

The judicial Power of the United States, shall be vested in one supreme Court, and in such inferior Courts as the Congress may from time to time ordain and establish. The Judges, both of the supreme and inferior Courts, shall hold their Offices during good Behaviour, and shall, at stated Times, receive for their Services, a Compensation, which shall not be diminished during their Continuance in Office.

Section 2.

Clause 1:
The judicial Power shall extend to all Cases, in Law and Equity, arising under this Constitution, the Laws of the United States, and Treaties made, or which shall be made, under their Authority; –to all Cases affecting Ambassadors, other public Ministers and Consuls; –to all Cases of admiralty and maritime Jurisdiction; –to Controversies to which the United States shall be a Party; –to Controversies between two or more States; –between a State and Citizens of another State; –between Citizens of different States, –between Citizens of the same State claiming Lands under Grants of different States, and between a State, or the Citizens thereof, and foreign States, Citizens or Subjects.

Clause 3:
The Trial of all Crimes, except in Cases of Impeachment, shall be by Jury; and such Trial shall be held in the State where the said Crimes shall have been committed; but when not committed within any State, the Trial shall be at such Place or Places as the Congress may by Law have directed.

—Article 3, U.S. Constitution

While the form of the government, representation in the legislature, and slavery were the most contentious issues, all the other points of the Virginia Plan were also debated, first in the Committee of the Whole, then in the convention, and finally in various committees appointed to resolve final issues. These discussions were responsible for the creation of the three separate branches of the new government—executive, legislative, and judicial—and the complicated system of checks and balances that was put in place to prevent any branch from assuming too much power.

The Legislature

Since the legislature had the power to make laws, the delegates spent most of the summer defining its role

and the limits of its authority. The resolution calling for a two-house legislature passed without major debate. Although some delegates, such as Benjamin Franklin, saw no reason to change the one-house Congress used during the confederation, the majority saw the wisdom in having two legislative houses to balance each other. When Thomas Jefferson returned from France and had breakfast with George Washington one day, he asked Washington why he wanted a bicameral legislature.

"Why did you pour that coffee into your saucer?" Washington asked him.

"To cool it," Jefferson answered.

"Even so," said Washington, "we pour legislation into the senatorial saucer to cool it."[1]

The resolution in the Virginia Plan that called for citizens to vote for members of the lower house caused a stir in the Committee of the Whole. Many delegates felt that ordinary people should have very little to do with the government. They believed that such people were not intelligent enough and lacked sufficient information to make wise decisions. Therefore, they believed, members of the House of Representatives should be elected by the state legislatures.

Other delegates had more faith in the people. James Madison considered it essential that at least one branch of the government be elected by popular vote. George Mason argued that the first house needed to "know and sympathize with every part of the community and ought, therefore, to be taken not only from different parts of the whole republic, but also from different districts of the larger members of it."[2] When the resolution was put to a vote in the Committee of the Whole, electing members of the House of Representatives by popular vote was approved by six states to two.

But the issue was not settled. Later in the convention, Gouverneur Morris moved that in order to vote for representatives in the lower house, people had to be landowners. Others immediately argued against such a restriction. Oliver Ellsworth warned, "The people will not readily subscribe to the national constitution if it should subject them to be disfranchised."[3] Benjamin Franklin was also against Morris's proposal. He did not think that the delegates had any right "to narrow the privileges of the electors."[4] When it went to a vote, the landowner requirement lost soundly, seven states to one.

After deciding that all the citizens would elect members of the lower house, the Committee of the Whole debated how to elect senators. The committee again was split into two groups: those delegates for election by the people, and those for election by the state legislatures. When the vote was taken, election of senators by state legislatures won. This decision held until 1913, when the Seventeenth Amendment allowed people to vote directly for their senators.

Many delegates wanted elections for legislators in the House to be held each year. Annual elections were "the only defense against tyranny," according to Elbridge Gerry.[5] However, Madison felt that representatives would need time to become informed about the office and national interests, and believed that a year was too short a time to be effective. He proposed three-year terms. The delegates compromised and decided upon two-year terms for members of the lower house. Delegates first gave members of the Senate seven-year terms. They also considered four, six, and nine years. Alexander Hamilton wanted the senators to be elected for life, as in the British House of Lords. The convention finally decided to make it a six-year term, with one-third of senators to be elected every two years.

Some delegates wanted the states to pay salaries to the representatives. Others, such as Alexander Hamilton, felt this would make the members of Congress "the mere agents and advocates of state interests and views."[6] The matter was undecided until August 14, when the convention decided that members should be paid out of the national treasury. The delegates also debated how much to pay the members of Congress. Finally they decided not to set a fixed amount. Instead, they gave Congress the authority to set its own pay by law.

The delegates all agreed that the new Congress should have more authority than the Confederation Congress. However, it was difficult to decide upon the additional powers and divide them between the House of Representatives and the Senate. Ultimately, the delegates gave the House the authority to originate money bills and the Senate the authority to accept or reject presidential appointments to executive and judicial offices. Other powers given to Congress included the right to levy and collect taxes; provide for the common defense and general welfare; borrow, coin, and regulate the value of money; regulate commerce; declare war; raise and support armies; admit new states; and impeach members of the executive and judicial branches.

One of the most important powers given to Congress was the authority "to make all laws which shall be necessary and proper for carrying into execution all the foregoing powers."[7] This is known as the elastic clause. The delegates at the Constitutional Convention knew they could not conceive of every power that Congress might need, so they wanted to build in a certain flexibility. The elastic clause has allowed Congress to make decisions regarding issues such as nuclear weapons and environmental concerns, which the Founding Fathers could not have foreseen.

The Executive

The executive branch challenged the delegates. There had been no executive under the Articles of Confederation, and the delegates still feared tyrannical leadership. This branch was in dispute until the very end of the convention.

Most of the delegates assumed that the respected George Washington would be the first executive of the nation, so they found it difficult to discuss the position openly in his presence. It seemed to them that any criticism of the office would be directed toward Washington himself. Benjamin Franklin sought to put them at ease. Because of his close friendship with Washington, the delegates respected his thoughts on the matter. The executive branch "is a point of great importance," he said. "I wish the gentlemen would deliver their sentiments on it

The inauguration of George Washington as the first president of the United States in Federal Hall in New York City. At right is a copy of the letter Washington wrote to Congress from Mount Vernon accepting the presidency.

before the question is put."[8] He also reminded them, "The first man put at the helm will be a good one. Nobody knows what sort may come afterwards."[9]

John Rutledge started the discussion in the Committee of the Whole by proclaiming, "I am for vesting the executive power in a single person . . . A single man will feel the greatest responsibility and administer the public affairs best."[10] Edmund Randolph feared a one-man executive would lead to a monarchy and proposed a three-man executive department. George Mason agreed and added that one of the three should come from the South, another from the middle states, and the third from the North.

James Wilson believed that three executives would be more trouble than the system was worth. He saw "nothing but uncontrolled, continued and violent animosities" among the three people.[11] He supported a single executive and felt that the people would know that a single magistrate was not the same as a king. His words were the last before the issue went to a vote. A single executive was agreed upon, seven states to three.

The issue of how to select the executive was also a difficult one—sixty votes were taken before the delegates reached a decision. First, they thought that Congress should elect the executive for a term of seven years with no possibility for reelection. Delegates who were against that idea feared that the process would make the president too indebted to Congress to fully check it. James Wilson wanted election by electors chosen by the people, but

Elbridge Gerry felt that the people were not wise enough to make good selections. Gerry in turn proposed that the governors of the states elect the president. This plan was also rejected. Several other methods were proposed and rejected before the issue went before the Committee on Postponed Matters.

The committee proposed that the executive be elected by electors who were voted for by the people. Each state would have the same number of electors as its number of representatives in the legislature. The candidate who received a majority of these electoral votes would become president, and the one with the next largest number of votes would become vice president. If the election was a tie or if there was no clear majority, the Senate would decide. Giving the Senate that much power made some delegates nervous. As a result, the final election of the president was moved from the Senate to the House of Representatives, with each state getting one vote. With these terms agreed upon, it was decided to give the executive a four-year term with the possibility of reelection. The Twenty-second Amendment later limited reelection to one additional term in office, and the Twelfth Amendment changed the manner in which the vice president was elected.

In the Virginia Plan, the executive received "a fixed compensation for services rendered." When the issue was discussed in the Committee of the Whole, Benjamin Franklin proposed instead that while the executive's expenses should be covered, presidents should "receive no salary, stipend fee or reward whatsoever for their services."[12] Franklin believed that if the position were to be paid, people would want the job for the money and not because they wanted to serve their country.

In his notes, Madison remarked that Franklin's ideas were debated out of respect for Franklin and not because the delegates felt them practical. Finally they agreed to the clause, "The President shall, at stated times, receive for his services, a compensation, which shall neither be increased or diminished during the period for which he shall have been elected, and he shall not receive within that period any other emolument from the United States, or any of them."[13]

Another important issue was the removal of the executive from office in the event of some egregious failure of responsibility or criminal behavior.

The Committee on Postponed Matters suggested that the Senate try all impeachment hearings with conviction requiring the agreement of two-thirds of the members. Pinckney opposed this suggestion because he feared that if the president "opposes a favorite law, the two Houses will combine against him, and under the influence of heat and faction throw him out."[14] Nonetheless, the convention decided upon removal of the president on impeachment by the House, trial by the Senate, and conviction dependent on a two-thirds vote. It also defined grounds for impeachment as treason, bribery, and other high crimes and misdemeanors. The vice president and other officers, such as federal judges, were also made impeachable.

The Committee on Postponed Matters also created the office of vice president in order to provide a position for the runner-up in the electoral vote. They decided that the vice president would serve as the president of Congress and vote only in the event of a tie. It was not clear that the vice president would take over presidential matters if the president died or became unable to perform his duties. John Tyler was the first vice president to assume the presidency after William Henry Harrison died in 1841. The practice was formally approved in 1967 with the passing of the Twenty-fifth Amendment.

The Judiciary

The judicial branch gave the delegates the least trouble. They knew they wanted a Supreme Court and federal circuit courts. But there was disagreement regarding the creation of lower, district courts. James Madison argued in favor of inferior courts because without them "appeals would be multiplied to an oppressive degree."[15] Others, however, felt that the circuit courts, instead of lower courts, should be the ones to give an initial decision. Roger Sherman was against creating lower courts because he felt it would be a burdensome expense. Other delegates felt district courts would save money by preventing numerous appeals to the Supreme Court.

In the end, the delegates agreed to disagree and left it up to Congress to decide. The first Congress passed the Judiciary Act of 1789, which set up the federal court system that the United States still has in place today. District courts are the first to try cases. The next level, circuit courts, hear cases that have been appealed from the lower courts. If the decision made by the circuit court is appealed, the case goes before the Supreme Court.

Many delegates wanted Congress to appoint federal judges for the states. Others thought that Congress would not be well qualified to make good selections. James Wilson argued that the executive should appoint judges because if Congress does there will be "intrigue, partiality, and concealment."[16] John Rutledge disagreed with Wilson. If the executive has the sole power, he warned, "the people will think we are leaning too much towards monarchy."[17] As the debate continued, Benjamin Franklin interjected with one of his tales and said that he had faith that the delegates could think of a similarly clever method. He told the delegates that in Scotland "the nomination proceeded from the lawyers, who always selected the ablest among the profession to get rid of him, and share his practice among themselves."[18] Although the appointment of judges by the executive was defeated on July 18, the delegates voted in September to give the president that authority. This decision was part of the compromise that moved the impeachment trials from the judiciary to the Senate.

John Dickinson felt that the president should have the authority to remove judges "on the application by the Senate and the House of Representatives."[19] Other delegates strongly disagreed. James Wilson argued that the judiciary would be severely weakened if judges were "made to depend on every gust of faction" that occurred in the executive and legislative branches.[20] In the end, the delegates decided that federal judges would remain in office "during good behavior," which basically meant they could stay on the bench until retirement or death. If a judge misbehaved, he or she could be impeached by the same method as the executive.

The Old Royal Exchange Building located at the foot of Broad Street, New York City. The Supreme Court held its first session here in 1790. At left is a portrait of John Jay, first chief justice of the Supreme Court.

Article VI of the Constitution states that the Constitution, the laws of the United States, and all treaties made under the authority of the United States "shall be the supreme law of the land; and the judges in every state shall be bound thereby."[21] While this statement does not explicitly spell out the role of judges, it has been agreed that judges have the power to decide if a national or state law is in accord with the Constitution.

Checks and Balances

In determining the various roles of the three branches, the delegates carefully balanced powers among them. They also developed a system in which the branches constantly check each other in order to prevent one group from becoming too powerful and controlling the others.

The executive branch, the office of the president, possesses a number of ways of checking the power of the legislative branch. First of all, the vice president is president of the Senate and can vote when there is a tie in the upper house. The president can also veto laws passed by the legislature, subject to legislative override of the veto. The president can call special sessions of Congress. The executive office can propose laws and can determine the federal budget. The executive office can fill vacancies for various administrative jobs that occur when the Senate is in recess. The executive branch also has some powers over the judicial branch. The president appoints federal judges, and the president can pardon people who have been convicted of federal crimes.

The legislative branch in turn has some checks on the executive branch. The House may impeach the president and other executive and judicial officials.

Impeachment hearings are tried in the Senate. Congress can override a presidential veto with a two-thirds vote of both the Senate and the House of Representatives. Congress must approve the federal budget. The Senate normally confirms presidential appointments, and the Senate approves treaties. Congress can also check the judicial branch. Congress determines the number, location, and jurisdiction of the federal lower courts. The Senate approves the appointment of judges. The House may impeach judges, and Congress can propose new legislation to overturn Supreme Court decisions.

The judicial branch can exercise checks on the power of the executive branch.

The chief justice of the Supreme Court presides at impeachment cases. The courts may declare executive orders unconstitutional. Judges are appointed for life and are free from executive control. Since the courts interpret the laws and their constitutionality, they also exercise a check on the power of the legislative branch.

Chapter Five

Ratification

> The Congress, whenever two thirds of both Houses shall deem it necessary, shall propose Amendments to this Constitution, or, on the Application of the Legislatures of two thirds of the several States, shall call a Convention for proposing Amendments, which, in either Case, shall be valid to all Intents and Purposes, as Part of this Constitution, when ratified by the Legislatures of three fourths of the several States, or by Conventions in three fourths thereof, as the one or the other Mode of Ratification may be proposed by the Congress; Provided that no Amendment which may be made prior to the Year One thousand eight hundred and eight shall in any Manner affect the first and fourth Clauses in the Ninth Section of the first Article; and that no State, without its Consent, shall be deprived of its equal Suffrage in the Senate.

—Article V, U.S. Constitution

After the three branches of government were in place, a Committee of Detail was appointed to draw up a complete draft of the Constitution. The committee was composed of John Rutledge, Edmund Randolph, Nathaniel Gorham, Oliver Ellsworth, and James Wilson. They met for two weeks, putting the various agreements and compromises into a concrete form. Documents such as the Iroquois Treaty of 1520, various state constitutions, the Virginia Plan, and the New Jersey Plan helped with their writing. Randolph presented the draft of the Constitution to the convention on August 6, 1787.

Final details were discussed and settled as the delegates examined the draft line by line. They could see the end of the convention approaching, which made them more agreeable to compromise. As the discussion wound down, a Committee of Style was appointed to put the document into its final form. The committee included Rufus King, James Madison, William Samuel Johnson, Gouverneur Morris, and Alexander Hamilton. On September 13, the Committee of Style presented the document to the convention. The Constitution was beautifully crafted—succinct and elegant, and written with style and grace.

The committee had greatly improved the preamble. The first version stated, "We the people of the States of…" and then listed all thirteen states. Many delegates felt that this opening didn't make sense because some states might refuse to ratify the document. Removing states from the list or adding them later would be awkward and distracting. Also, they wondered what would happen when new states entered the Union. The problem was solved when the committee simplified the preamble with the phrase, "We the people of the United States." The change also more strongly expressed that the people were going to be the government's foundation, not the states.

George Mason brought up the lack of a bill of rights at this point. He felt one was of vital importance to the Constitution and offered to write it. Elbridge Gerry agreed with the idea. But the other delegates, perhaps tired of the convention and ready to go home, voted against the idea. Roger Sherman told them that the states' rights "are not repealed by this Constitution, and being in force are sufficient."[1] Mason argued that if the Constitution were made the supreme law of the land, it would override all the states' bills of rights, leaving citizens unprotected. Nonetheless, a bill of rights was unanimously voted down.

With no further alterations, the version created by the Committee of Style was approved on September 15, four months after Madison and the Virginia delegates began writing the Virginia Plan. When the states were asked whether they agreed to the Constitution, they all answered in unison: "Ay!"[2]

The first page of the original handwritten draft of the Constitution of the United States. The prominent use of the phrase "We the People" was symbolic of John Locke's social contract theory, which declared that governments ruled with the consent of their citizens.

Signing the Constitution

The convention assembled for the last time on September 17, 1787. The final version of the Constitution was read to the forty-one delegates present. The number of compromises that had taken place had produced a document that no one was thrilled with, but one most thought was the best they could do.

When the reading was completed, Benjamin Franklin gave a speech expressing his approval of the Constitution. He requested, "Every member of the Convention who may still have objections to it would with me, on this occasion, doubt a little of his own infallibility and, to make manifest our unanimity, put his name to this instrument."[3]

Despite the request, not all of the delegates felt that they could sign it. Edmund Randolph, who had presented the Virginia Plan to the convention, felt that "indefinite and dangerous power" had been given to the Congress.[4] He declared that he would sign the document only if the states were able to review it first and propose changes at another convention. James Wilson voiced the opinion of most delegates when he said in exasperation, "After spending four or five months in the laborious and arduous task of forming a government for our country, we are ourselves at the close throwing insuperable obstacles in the way of its success."[5] Nevertheless, Randolph would not support a constitution that he felt would "end in tyranny."[6]

George Mason still insisted on a bill of rights. He feared that without one Americans' fundamental rights would be put in jeopardy. He claimed, "I would rather chop off my right hand than put it to the Constitution as it now stands."[7] He also felt that the government was going to be an aristocracy in which the privileged few would rule over the many. "This constitution," he declared, "has been formed without the knowledge or idea of the people. A second convention will know more of the sense of the people, and be able to provide a system more consonant to it. It was improper to say to the people, take this or nothing."[8]

Elbridge Gerry was the last delegate present who refused to sign the Constitution. He had a number of doubts about the system of government, the most important one being that the rights of citizens were insecure. He also wanted the people to have a chance to make recommendations and requested that another convention be held. After four months of bickering and arguing, sweating in a stuffy room, and being away from their families and livelihoods, it is not surprising

that the delegates shouted down the motion for a second convention.

Franklin's speech, however, moved all the other delegates, and they lined up according to state to sign the Constitution. As the last few delegates signed their names, Franklin remarked that he had often gazed upon the high-back chair and wondered whether the carved sun was rising or setting. He continued, "Now at length I have the happiness to know that it is a rising and not a setting sun."[9] Indeed, the sun would soon rise over the new government of the United

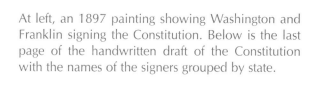

At left, an 1897 painting showing Washington and Franklin signing the Constitution. Below is the last page of the handwritten draft of the Constitution with the names of the signers grouped by state.

States. But, before that happened, the delegates faced another challenge. They had to convince the people to make their plan a reality.

The Ratification Process

In planning how to ratify the document, the delegates knew that if they sent it to the state legislatures, it would never pass. Instead, they determined that the people of each state would select electors to vote on the Constitution at ratifying conventions.

The need for all thirteen states to approve any change to the Articles of Confederation had been a major obstacle in fixing the government. Since Rhode Island had refused even to attend the Constitutional Convention, the delegates knew they would never get unanimous acceptance. So they created an article in the Constitution stating that only nine states needed to ratify the document for it to take effect. On September 28, 1787, the Constitution was sent to the states, and the fight for ratification began.

Those who supported the Constitution at this time were called Federalists. Those opposed to the Constitution became known as Antifederalists. As soon as they left the convention, Federalists and Antifederalists made their views known. Federalists pointed out the strengths of the new government and showed how the Constitution fixed the defects of the Articles of Confederation. Antifederalists objected to the lack of a bill of rights. Without a bill of rights, they claimed that the new government could take away many personal liberties. They were also concerned that the proposed government would destroy state sovereignty and that the executive would create a monarchy.

Just two weeks after the Constitutional Convention ended, Federalists in the Pennsylvania Assembly requested a date be determined for the ratifying convention. They hoped to have the distinction of being the first state to ratify. A quorum of forty-seven delegates was needed to set the date, so the Antifederalists boycotted the meeting, leaving the assembly two delegates short. The sergeant at arms located two Antifederalists and, with the help of Federalist supporters, dragged them through the streets to the meeting. With the quorum, the assembly quickly voted 45 to 2 to hold the ratifying convention on the first Tuesday of November. At Pennsylvania's ratification convention, the discussions were long and intense. Finally, by a vote of 43 to 23, the Pennsylvania convention accepted the Constitution on December 12.

Despite Pennsylvania's rush, it was not the first state to join the Union. On December 7, 1787, Delaware's ratifying convention approved the Constitution unanimously. The next two states to ratify were New Jersey and Georgia. Both conventions voted unanimously to accept the Constitution. Connecticut soon followed with a vote of 128 to 40. So far, five states had voted to ratify. Four more were needed for the Constitution to go into effect.

Massachusetts's ratifying convention began on January 9, 1788. The majority of delegates at the convention were strong Antifederalists whose main argument against the Constitution was the lack of a bill of rights. The governor of Massachusetts, John Hancock, was not sure which side to support. The Federalists appealed to his ego by saying that if Virginia failed to ratify, making George Washington ineligible for the presidency, he could become the nation's first president. The flattery worked, and Hancock came out in support of the Constitution. As a result, on February 6, Massachusetts became the sixth state to accept the Constitution by a vote of 187 to 168.

Maryland and South Carolina were the next states to ratify the Constitution, and both accepted it by large margins. Now eight states had voted to ratify—one short of the necessary nine. The Federalists knew, however, that the last vote would be the hardest to get. Rhode Island would never accept it; the state hadn't even attended the Philadelphia Convention. North Carolina also appeared to be strongly against the Constitution. Hope rested on Virginia, New Hampshire, and New York.

The Virginia convention opened on June 2, 1788. The Antifederalists included many important men, such as Patrick Henry, George Mason, and Richard Henry Lee. They demanded that the convention introduce a bill of rights and postpone the adoption of the Constitution until each state accepted the new amendments. The Federalists argued that the request was unreasonable. Eight states had already ratified the Constitution as it was. Requiring the approval of a new bill of rights would force them to repeat their ratifying conventions. The Federalists did, however, promise that the first act of the new Congress would be to propose a series of amendments to the Constitution.

This promise and the fact that the revolutionary war hero George Washington supported the Constitution helped sway many Virginia Antifederalists to the Federalist side. Edmund Randolph, who had refused to sign the Constitution, changed his mind and now supported the document. Pointing to his arm, he dramatically declared, "I would assent to the lopping of this limb before I assent to the dissolution of the Union."[10]

Before the Virginia convention could vote, however, the delegates received the news that New Hampshire had become the ninth state to ratify the Constitution on June 21. Now it didn't matter what Virginia decided. The Articles of Confederation were dead and the new government had been born.

Virginia anticlimactically ratified the Constitution four days after New Hampshire.

Although the Constitution had been ratified, it was still important to get New York on board. New York City was a major center for trade, and without the state New England would be cut off from the rest of the Union. The delegates for the New York convention had assembled on June 17, 1788, while New Hampshire and Virginia were meeting. The Antifederalists were determined to force a second national convention to revise the Constitution.

The Federalists' cause, however, had been helped by a series of eighty-five letters that appeared in New York newspapers. They were signed "Publius" (a Roman leader who had established a stable government) and clearly spelled out how the new government would work and promoted its ratification. The real authors of these letters were Alexander Hamilton, James Madison, and John Jay, a New Yorker who had been president of the Continental Congress. In May 1788, the letters were published in a book titled *The Federalist*. Today, the letters are regarded as some of the best writing on the Constitution and are widely read and studied.

Another thing that helped the Federalists was the rumor that if the New York convention refused to ratify, New York City would secede and join the union. Also, the news that New Hampshire and Virginia had ratified the Constitution began to wear down the Antifederalists. On July 26, the New York convention agreed to ratify the Constitution by a narrow vote of 30 to 27.

North Carolina and Rhode Island both rejected the Constitution, as expected. But few people worried about that fact. The new Union could survive without those two states, and they would essentially become foreign countries. On November 19, 1789, North Carolina decided it could not exist safely apart from the Union, so a second convention was held and the electors voted to ratify the Constitution. Rhode Island stubbornly held out a little longer. It was not until May 1790, when the Senate passed a bill ending trade with Rhode Island, that it joined the union.

The New United States of America

The Constitution went into effect on March 4, 1789, and the nation's first capital was established in New York City. The state electors unanimously elected George Washington as the first president. On December 15, 1791, the first ten amendments were

The first capital of the United States was New York City. Pictured here is Federal Hall in lower Manhattan, where the first Congress met in 1789.

added to the Constitution, remedying the lack of a bill of rights. The personal liberties of all Americans were secured by guarantees of free speech, a free press, freedom of religion, and due process. Throughout the years, seventeen more amendments have been added.

Praising the Constitution, Benjamin Rush wrote to John Adams, "It has a thousand things to recommend it. It makes us a nation. It rescues us from anarchy and slavery. It revives agriculture and commerce. It checks moral and political iniquity. In a word, it makes a man both willing to live and to die. To live, because it opens to him fair prospects of great public and private happiness. To die, because it ensures peace, order, safety, and prosperity to his children."[11]

The Constitution of the United States

PREAMBLE.

We the People of the United States, in Order to form a more perfect Union, establish Justice, insure domestic tranquility, provide for the common defence, promote the general Welfare, and secure the Blessings of Liberty to ourselves and our Posterity, do ordain and establish this Constitution for the United States of America.

Article I.

Section 1.

All legislative Powers herein granted shall be vested in a Congress of the United States, which shall consist of a Senate and House of Representatives.

Section 2.

Clause 1:
The House of Representatives shall be composed of Members chosen every second Year by the People of

the several States, and the Electors in each State shall have the Qualifications requisite for Electors of the most numerous Branch of the State Legislature.

Clause 2:
No Person shall be a Representative who shall not have attained to the Age of twenty five Years, and been seven Years a Citizen of the United States, and who shall not, when elected, be an Inhabitant of that State in which he shall be chosen.

Clause 3:
Representatives and direct Taxes shall be apportioned among the several States which may be included within this Union, according to their respective Numbers, which shall be determined by adding to the whole Number of free Persons, including those bound to Service for a Term of Years, and excluding Indians not taxed, three fifths of all other Persons. The actual Enumeration shall be made within three Years after the first Meeting of the Congress of the United States, and within every subsequent Term of ten Years, in such Manner as they shall by Law direct. The Number of Representatives shall not exceed one for every thirty Thousand, but each State shall have at Least one Representative; and until such enumeration shall be made, the State of New Hampshire shall be entitled to chuse three, Massachusetts eight, Rhode Island and Providence Plantations one, Connecticut five, New

York six, New Jersey four, Pennsylvania eight, Delaware one, Maryland six, Virginia ten, North Carolina five, South Carolina five, and Georgia three.

Clause 4:
When vacancies happen in the Representation from any State, the Executive Authority thereof shall issue Writs of Election to fill such Vacancies.

Clause 5:
The House of Representatives shall chuse their Speaker and other Officers; and shall have the sole Power of Impeachment.

Section 3.

Clause 1:
The Senate of the United States shall be composed of two Senators from each State, chosen by the Legislature thereof, for six Years; and each Senator shall have one Vote.

Clause 2:
Immediately after they shall be assembled in Consequence of the first Election, they shall be divided as equally as may be into three Classes. The Seats of the Senators of the first Class shall be vacated at the Expiration of the second Year, of the second Class at the Expiration of the fourth Year, and of the third Class at the Expiration of the sixth Year, so that one third may

be chosen every second Year; and if Vacancies happen by Resignation, or otherwise, during the Recess of the Legislature of any State, the Executive thereof may make temporary Appointments until the next Meeting of the Legislature, which shall then fill such Vacancies.

Clause 3:
No Person shall be a Senator who shall not have attained to the Age of thirty Years, and been nine Years a Citizen of the United States, and who shall not, when elected, be an Inhabitant of that State for which he shall be chosen.

Clause 4:
The Vice President of the United States shall be President of the Senate, but shall have no Vote, unless they be equally divided.

Clause 5:

The Senate shall chuse their other Officers, and also a President pro tempore, in the Absence of the Vice President, or when he shall exercise the Office of President of the United States.

Clause 6:
The Senate shall have the sole Power to try all Impeachments. When sitting for that Purpose, they shall be on Oath or Affirmation. When the President of the United States is tried, the Chief Justice shall preside:

And no Person shall be convicted without the Concurrence of two thirds of the Members present.

Clause 7:
Judgment in Cases of Impeachment shall not extend further than to removal from Office, and disqualification to hold and enjoy any Office of honor, Trust or Profit under the United States: but the Party convicted shall nevertheless be liable and subject to Indictment, Trial, Judgment and Punishment, according to Law.

Section 4.

Clause 1:
The Times, Places and Manner of holding Elections for Senators and Representatives, shall be prescribed in each State by the Legislature thereof; but the Congress may at any time by Law make or alter such Regulations, except as to the Places of chusing Senators.

Clause 2:
The Congress shall assemble at least once in every Year, and such Meeting shall be on the first Monday in December, unless they shall by Law appoint a different Day.

Section 5.

Clause 1:
Each House shall be the Judge of the Elections, Returns and Qualifications of its own Members,

and a Majority of each shall constitute a Quorum to do Business; but a smaller Number may adjourn from day to day, and may be authorized to compel the Attendance of absent Members, in such Manner, and under such Penalties as each House may provide.

Clause 2:
Each House may determine the Rules of its Proceedings, punish its Members for disorderly Behaviour, and, with the Concurrence of two thirds, expel a Member.

Clause 3:
Each House shall keep a Journal of its Proceedings, and from time to time publish the same, excepting such Parts as may in their Judgment require Secrecy; and the Yeas and Nays of the Members of either House on any question shall, at the Desire of one fifth of those Present, be entered on the Journal.

Clause 4:
Neither House, during the Session of Congress, shall, without the Consent of the other, adjourn for more than three days, nor to any other Place than that in which the two Houses shall be sitting.

Section 6.

Clause 1:
The Senators and Representatives shall receive a Compensation for their Services, to be ascertained by

Law, and paid out of the Treasury of the United States. They shall in all Cases, except Treason, Felony and Breach of the Peace, be privileged from Arrest during their Attendance at the Session of their respective Houses, and in going to and returning from the same; and for any Speech or Debate in either House, they shall not be questioned in any other Place.

Clause 2:
No Senator or Representative shall, during the Time for which he was elected, be appointed to any civil Office under the Authority of the United States, which shall have been created, or the Emoluments whereof shall have been increased during such time; and no Person holding any Office under the United States, shall be a Member of either House during his Continuance in Office.

Section 7.

Clause 1:
All Bills for raising Revenue shall originate in the House of Representatives; but the Senate may pro-pose or concur with Amendments as on other Bills.

Clause 2:
Every Bill which shall have passed the House of Representatives and the Senate, shall, before it become a Law, be presented to the President of the United States; If he approve he shall sign it, but if

not he shall return it, with his Objections to that House in which it shall have originated, who shall enter the Objections at large on their Journal, and proceed to reconsider it. If after such Reconsideration two thirds of that House shall agree to pass the Bill, it shall be sent, together with the Objections, to the other House, by which it shall likewise be reconsidered, and if approved by two thirds of that House, it shall become a Law. But in all such Cases the Votes of both Houses shall be determined by yeas and Nays, and the Names of the Persons voting for and against the Bill shall be entered on the Journal of each House respectively. If any Bill shall not be returned by the President within ten Days (Sundays excepted) after it shall have been presented to him, the Same shall be a Law, in like Manner as if he had signed it, unless the Congress by their Adjournment prevent its Return, in which Case it shall not be a Law.

Clause 3:
Every Order, Resolution, or Vote to which the Concurrence of the Senate and House of Representatives may be necessary (except on a question of Adjournment) shall be presented to the President of the United States; and before the Same shall take Effect, shall be approved by him, or being disapproved by him, shall be repassed by two thirds of the Senate and House of Representatives, according to the Rules and Limitations prescribed in the Case of a Bill.

Section 8.

Clause 1:
The Congress shall have Power To lay and collect Taxes, Duties, Imposts and Excises, to pay the Debts and provide for the common Defence and general Welfare of the United States; but all Duties, Imposts and Excises shall be uniform throughout the United States;

Clause 2:
To borrow Money on the credit of the United States;

Clause 3:
To regulate Commerce with foreign Nations, and among the several States, and with the Indian Tribes;

Clause 4:
To establish a uniform Rule of Naturalization, and uniform Laws on the subject of Bankruptcies through-out the United States;

Clause 5:
To coin Money, regulate the Value thereof, and of foreign Coin, and fix the Standard of Weights and Measures;

Clause 6:
To provide for the Punishment of counterfeiting the Securities and current Coin of the United States;

Clause 7:
To establish Post Offices and post Roads;

Clause 8:
To promote the Progress of Science and useful Arts, by securing for limited Times to Authors and Inventors the exclusive Right to their respective Writings and Discoveries;

Clause 9:
To constitute Tribunals inferior to the supreme Court;

Clause 10:
To define and punish Piracies and Felonies committed on the high Seas, and Offences against the Law of Nations;

Clause 11:
To declare War, grant Letters of Marque and Reprisal, and make Rules concerning Captures on Land and Water;

Clause 12:
To raise and support Armies, but no Appropriation of Money to that Use shall be for a longer Term than two Years;

Clause 13:
To provide and maintain a Navy;

Clause 14:
To make Rules for the Government and Regulation of the land and naval Forces;

Clause 15:
To provide for calling forth the Militia to execute the Laws of the Union, suppress Insurrections and repel Invasions;

Clause 16:
To provide for organizing, arming, and disciplining, the Militia, and for governing such Part of them as may be employed in the Service of the United States, reserving to the States respectively, the Appointment of the Officers, and the Authority of training the Militia according to the discipline prescribed by Congress;

Clause 17:
To exercise exclusive Legislation in all Cases whatsoever, over such District (not exceeding ten Miles square) as may, by Cession of particular States, and the Acceptance of Congress, become the Seat of the Government of the United States, and to exercise like Authority over all Places purchased by the Consent of the Legislature of the State in which the Same shall be, for the Erection of Forts, Magazines, Arsenals, dock-Yards, and other needful Buildings; –And

Clause 18:
To make all Laws which shall be necessary and proper for carrying into Execution the foregoing Powers, and all other Powers vested by this Constitution in the Government of the United States, or in any Department or Officer thereof.

Section 9.

Clause 1:
The Migration or Importation of such Persons as any of the States now existing shall think proper to admit, shall not be prohibited by the Congress prior to the Year one thousand eight hundred and eight, but a Tax or duty may be imposed on such Importation, not exceeding ten dollars for each Person.

Clause 2:
The Privilege of the Writ of Habeas Corpus shall not be suspended, unless when in Cases of Rebellion or Invasion the public Safety may require it.

Clause 3:
No Bill of Attainder or ex post facto Law shall be passed.

Clause 4:
No Capitation, or other direct, Tax shall be laid, unless in Proportion to the Census or Enumeration herein before directed to be taken.

Clause 5:
No Tax or Duty shall be laid on Articles exported from any State.

Clause 6:
No Preference shall be given by any Regulation of Commerce or Revenue to the Ports of one State

over those of another: nor shall Vessels bound to, or from, one State, be obliged to enter, clear, or pay Duties in another.

Clause 7:
No Money shall be drawn from the Treasury, but in Consequence of Appropriations made by Law; and a regular Statement and Account of the Receipts and Expenditures of all public Money shall be published from time to time.

Clause 8:
No Title of Nobility shall be granted by the United States: And no Person holding any Office of Profit or Trust under them, shall, without the Consent of the Congress, accept of any present, Emolument, Office, or Title, of any kind whatever, from any King, Prince, or foreign State.

Section 10.

Clause 1:
No State shall enter into any Treaty, Alliance, or Confederation; grant Letters of Marque and Reprisal; coin Money; emit Bills of Credit; make any Thing but gold and silver Coin a Tender in Payment of Debts; pass any Bill of Attainder, ex post facto Law, or Law impairing the Obligation of Contracts, or grant any Title of Nobility.

Clause 2:
No State shall, without the Consent of the Congress, lay any Imposts or Duties on Imports or Exports, except what may be absolutely necessary for executing its inspection Laws: and the net Produce of all Duties and Imposts, laid by any State on Imports or Exports, shall be for the Use of the Treasury of the United States; and all such Laws shall be subject to the Revision and Controul of the Congress.

Clause 3:
No State shall, without the Consent of Congress, lay any Duty of Tonnage, keep Troops, or Ships of War in time of Peace, enter into any Agreement or Compact with another State, or with a foreign Power, or engage in War, unless actually invaded, or in such imminent Danger as will not admit of delay.

Article II.

Section 1.

Clause 1:
The executive Power shall be vested in a President of the United States of America. He shall hold his Office during the Term of four Years, and, together with the Vice President, chosen for the same Term, be elected, as follows:

Clause 2:
Each State shall appoint, in such Manner as the Legislature thereof may direct, a Number of Electors, equal to the whole Number of Senators and Representatives to which the State may be entitled in the Congress: but no Senator or Representative, or Person holding an Office of Trust or Profit under the United States, shall be appointed an Elector.

Clause 3:
The Electors shall meet in their respective States, and vote by Ballot for two Persons, of whom one at least shall not be an Inhabitant of the same State with themselves. And they shall make a List of all the Persons voted for, and of the Number of Votes for each; which List they shall sign and certify, and transmit sealed to the Seat of the Government of the United States, directed to the President of the Senate. The President of the Senate shall, in the Presence of the Senate and House of Representatives, open all the Certificates, and the Votes shall then be counted. The Person having the greatest Number of Votes shall be the President, if such Number be a Majority of the whole Number of Electors appointed; and if there be more than one who have such Majority, and have an equal Number of Votes, then the House of Representatives shall immediately chuse by Ballot one of them for President; and if no Person have a Majority, then from the five highest on the List the said House shall in like Manner chuse the President. But in chusing the

President, the Votes shall be taken by States, the Representation from each State having one Vote; A quorum for this Purpose shall consist of a Member or Members from two thirds of the States, and a Majority of all the States shall be necessary to a Choice. In every Case, after the Choice of the President, the Person having the greatest Number of Votes of the Electors shall be the Vice President. But if there should remain two or more who have equal Votes, the Senate shall chuse from them by Ballot the Vice President.

Clause 4:
The Congress may determine the Time of choosing the Electors, and the Day on which they shall give their Votes; which Day shall be the same throughout the United States.

Clause 5:
No Person except a natural born Citizen, or a Citizen of the United States, at the time of the Adoption of this Constitution, shall be eligible to the Office of President; neither shall any Person be eligible to that Office who shall not have attained to the Age of thirty five Years, and been fourteen Years a Resident within the United States.

Clause 6:
In Case of the Removal of the President from Office, or of his Death, Resignation, or Inability to discharge the Powers and Duties of the said Office, the Same shall

devolve on the Vice President, and the Congress may by Law provide for the Case of Removal, Death, Resignation or Inability, both of the President and Vice President, declaring what Officer shall then act as President, and such Officer shall act accordingly, until the Disability be removed, or a President shall be elected.

Clause 7:
The President shall, at stated Times, receive for his Services, a Compensation, which shall neither be encreased nor diminished during the Period for which he shall have been elected, and he shall not receive within that Period any other Emolument from the United States, or any of them.

Clause 8:
Before he enter on the Execution of his Office, he shall take the following Oath or Affirmation:–"I do solemnly swear (or affirm) that I will faithfully execute the Office of President of the United States, and will to the best of my Ability, preserve, protect and defend the Constitution of the United States."

Section 2.

Clause 1:
The President shall be Commander in Chief of the Army and Navy of the United States, and of the Militia of the several States, when called into the actual Service of the United States; he may require the Opinion, in writing,

of the principal Officer in each of the executive Departments, upon any Subject relating to the Duties of their respective Offices, and he shall have Power to grant Reprieves and Pardons for Offences against the United States, except in Cases of Impeachment.

Clause 2:
He shall have Power, by and with the Advice and Consent of the Senate, to make Treaties, provided two thirds of the Senators present concur; and he shall nominate, and by and with the Advice and Consent of the Senate, shall appoint Ambassadors, other public Ministers and Consuls, Judges of the supreme Court, and all other Officers of the United States, whose Appointments are not herein otherwise provided for, and which shall be established by Law: but the Congress may by Law vest the Appointment of such inferior Officers, as they think proper, in the President alone, in the Courts of Law, or in the Heads of Departments.

Clause 3:
The President shall have Power to fill up all Vacancies that may happen during the Recess of the Senate, by granting Commissions which shall expire at the End of their next Session.

Section 3.

He shall from time to time give to the Congress Information of the State of the Union, and recommend to their Consideration such Measures as he shall judge necessary and expedient; he may, on extraordinary Occasions, convene both Houses, or either of them, and in Case of Disagreement between them, with Respect to the Time of Adjournment, he may adjourn them to such Time as he shall think proper; he shall receive Ambassadors and other public Ministers; he shall take Care that the Laws be faithfully executed, and shall Commission all the Officers of the United States.

Section 4.

The President, Vice President and all civil Officers of the United States, shall be removed from Office on Impeachment for, and Conviction of, Treason, Bribery, or other high Crimes and Misdemeanors.

Article III.

Section 1.

The judicial Power of the United States, shall be vested in one supreme Court, and in such inferior Courts as the Congress may from time to time ordain and establish. The Judges, both of the supreme and inferior Courts, shall hold their Offices during good Behaviour, and shall, at stated Times, receive for their Services, a Compensation, which shall not be diminished during their Continuance in Office.

Section 2.

Clause 1:
The judicial Power shall extend to all Cases, in Law and Equity, arising under this Constitution, the Laws of the United States, and Treaties made, or which shall be made, under their Authority; –to all Cases affecting Ambassadors, other public Ministers and Consuls; –to all Cases of admiralty and maritime Jurisdiction; –to Controversies to which the United States shall be a Party; –to Controversies between two or more States; –between a State and Citizens of another State; –between Citizens of different States, –between Citizens of the same State claiming Lands under Grants of different States, and between a State, or the Citizens thereof, and foreign States, Citizens or Subjects.

Clause 2:
In all Cases affecting Ambassadors, other public Ministers and Consuls, and those in which a State shall be Party, the supreme Court shall have original Jurisdiction. In all the other Cases before mentioned, the supreme Court shall have appellate Jurisdiction, both as to Law and Fact, with such Exceptions, and under such Regulations as the Congress shall make.

Clause 3:
The Trial of all Crimes, except in Cases of Impeachment, shall be by Jury; and such Trial shall

be held in the State where the said Crimes shall have been committed; but when not committed within any State, the Trial shall be at such Place or Places as the Congress may by Law have directed.

Section 3.

Clause 1:
Treason against the United States, shall consist only in levying War against them, or in adhering to their Enemies, giving them Aid and Comfort. No Person shall be convicted of Treason unless on the Testimony of two Witnesses to the same overt Act, or on Confession in open Court.

Clause 2:
The Congress shall have Power to declare the Punishment of Treason, but no Attainder of Treason shall work Corruption of Blood, or Forfeiture except during the Life of the Person attainted.

Article IV.
Section 1.

Full Faith and Credit shall be given in each State to the public Acts, Records, and judicial Proceedings of every other State. And the Congress may by general Laws prescribe the Manner in which such Acts, Records and Proceedings shall be proved, and the Effect thereof.

Section 2.

Clause 1:
The Citizens of each State shall be entitled to all Privileges and Immunities of Citizens in the several States.

Clause 2:
A Person charged in any State with Treason, Felony, or other Crime, who shall flee from Justice, and be found in another State, shall on Demand of the executive Authority of the State from which he fled, be delivered up, to be removed to the State having Jurisdiction of the Crime.

Clause 3:
No Person held to Service or Labour in one State, under the Laws thereof, escaping into another, shall, in Consequence of any Law or Regulation therein, be discharged from such Service or Labour, but shall be delivered up on Claim of the Party to whom such Service or Labour may be due.

Section 3.

Clause 1:
New States may be admitted by the Congress into this Union; but no new State shall be formed or erected within the Jurisdiction of any other State; nor any State be formed by the Junction of two or more States, or

Parts of States, without the Consent of the Legislatures of the States concerned as well as of the Congress.

Clause 2:
The Congress shall have Power to dispose of and make all needful Rules and Regulations respecting the Territory or other Property belonging to the United States; and nothing in this Constitution shall be so construed as to Prejudice any Claims of the United States, or of any particular State.

Section 4.

The United States shall guarantee to every State in this Union a Republican Form of Government, and shall protect each of them against Invasion; and on Application of the Legislature, or of the Executive (when the Legislature cannot be convened) against domestic Violence.

Article V.

The Congress, whenever two thirds of both Houses shall deem it necessary, shall propose Amendments to this Constitution, or, on the Application of the Legislatures of two thirds of the several States, shall call a Convention for proposing Amendments, which, in either Case, shall be valid to all Intents and Purposes, as Part of this Constitution, when ratified by the Legislatures of three fourths of the several States, or by Conventions in three fourths thereof, as the one or the other Mode of Ratification may be proposed by the Congress; Provided that no Amendment which may be made prior to the Year One thousand eight hundred and eight shall in any Manner affect the first and fourth Clauses in the Ninth Section of the first Article; and that no State, without its Consent, shall be deprived of its equal Suffrage in the Senate.

Article VI.

Clause 1:
All Debts contracted and Engagements entered into, before the Adoption of this Constitution, shall be as valid against the United States under this Constitution, as under the Confederation.

Clause 2:
This Constitution, and the Laws of the United States which shall be made in Pursuance thereof; and all Treaties made, or which shall be made, under the Authority of the United States, shall be the supreme Law of the Land; and the Judges in every State shall be bound thereby, any Thing in the Constitution or Laws of any State to the Contrary notwithstanding.

Clause 3:
The Senators and Representatives before mentioned, and the Members of the several State Legislatures, and all executive and judicial Officers, both of the

United States and of the several States, shall be bound by Oath or Affirmation, to support this Constitution; but no religious Test shall ever be required as a Qualification to any Office or public Trust under the United States.

Article VII.

The Ratification of the Conventions of nine States, shall be sufficient for the Establishment of this Constitution between the States so ratifying the Same.

Done in Convention by the Unanimous Consent of the States present the Seventeenth Day of September in the Year of our Lord one thousand seven hundred and Eighty seven and of the Independence of the United States of America the Twelfth In witness whereof We have hereunto subscribed our Names, George Washington

Presidt. and deputy from Virginia

New Hampshire
John Langdon
Nicholas Gilman

Delaware
Geo. Read
Gunning Bedford jun
John Dickinson

Richard Bassett
Jaco: Broom

Massachusetts
Nathaniel Gorham
Rufus King

Maryland
James MCHenry
Dan: of St. Thos. Jenifer
Danl Carroll

Connecticut
Wm. Saml. Johnson
Roger Sherman

Virginia
John Blair
James Madison Jr.

New Jersey
Wil: Livingston
David Brearley.
Wm. Paterson.
Jona: Dayton

North Carolina
Wm. Blount
Richd. Dobbs Spaight.
Hu Williamson

Pennsylvania
B Franklin
Thomas Mifflin
Robt. Morris
Geo. Clymer
Thos. FitzSimons
Jared Ingersoll
James Wilson
Gouv Morris

South Carolina
J. Rutledge
Charles Cotesworth Pinckney
Charles Pinckney
Pierce Butler

Georgia
William Few
Abr Baldwin

Attest:
William Jackson, Secretary

Glossary

amendment An alteration or addition to a document. The U.S. Constitution has had twenty-seven amendments added to it. The first ten are known as the Bill of Rights.

Antifederalist A person who opposed ratification of the U.S. Constitution. Those in favor of it were called Federalists. Antifederalists wanted a weak national government and strong state governments.

Articles of Confederation The document, ratified in 1777, that established the first plan of government in the United States. It gave the states a great deal of power and limited the role of the national government. It was replaced by the Constitution in 1789.

bicameral A legislative system composed of two houses. The two houses of the U.S. Congress are the House of Representatives and the Senate.

Bill of Rights The first ten amendments to the U.S. Constitution. They were ratified in 1791.

Committee of the Whole The group used by the Constitutional Convention to allow free debate and nonbinding votes. It was also used by Britain's House of Commons.

constitution A nation's basic law. It outlines the powers of the government and describes how those powers are to be used.

democracy A form of government in which the people themselves decide who has political power.

elector A person chosen to represent many in the election of the president.

executive The branch of the government that carries out the laws made by the legislature.

faction A group of people with similar interests joined together to promote their political views.

Magna Carta The English document that stated that a king cannot encroach on the fundamental rights of his subjects.

monarchy A nation or state governed by one person. At the time of the Revolutionary War, England was a monarchy ruled by King George III.

ratify To approve and accept. Treaties and constitutions must be ratified by Congress before they go into effect.

republic A form of government that gets its power, directly or indirectly, from the people. In a republic, people select representatives who make the laws.

sovereignty The power to govern without external control. In declaring their sovereignty under the Articles of Confederation, the states remained independent and kept most of their powers, while the central government was weak.

suffrage The right to vote.

Treaty of Paris The document that officially ended the Revolutionary War. It was ratified in 1783.

For More Information

American Historical Association
400 A Street SE
Washington, DC 20003-3889
(202) 544-2422
Web site: http://www.theaha.org

American Historical Review
Indiana University
914 Atwater Avenue
Bloomington, IN 47401
(812) 855-7609
Web site: http://www.historycooperative.org/ahr

American Independence Museum
One Governor's Lane
Exeter, NH 03833
(603) 772-2622
Web site: http://www.independencemuseum.org

The Library of Congress
101 Independence Avenue SE
Washington, DC 20540
(202) 707-5000
Web site: http://www.loc.gov

Smithsonian Institution
P.O. Box 37012
SI Building, Room 153, MRC 010
Washington, DC 20013-7012
(202) 357-2020
Web site: http://www.smithsonian.org

Web Sites

Due to the changing nature of Internet links, the Rosen Publishing Group, Inc., has developed an online list of Web sites related to the subject of this book. This site is updated regularly. Please use this link to access the list:

http://www.rosenlinks.com/gapd/usco/

For Further Reading

Agel, Jerome, and Mort Gerberg. *The U.S. Constitution for Everyone.* New York: Berkley Publishing Group, 1987.

Bjornlund, Lydia. *The U.S. Constitution: Blueprint for Democracy.* San Diego: Lucent Books, 1999.

Bowen, Catherine Drinker. *Miracle at Philadelphia.* Boston: Little, Brown and Company, 1966.

Cullop, Floyd G. *The Constitution of the United States: An Introduction.* New York: New American Library, 1999.

Haesly, Richard, ed. *The Constitutional Convention.* San Diego: Greenhaven Press, 2002.

Lindop, Edmund. *Birth of the Constitution.* Springfield, NJ: Enslow Publishers, 1987.

Mee, Charles L., Jr. *The Genius of the People.* New York: Harper and Row, 1987.

Mitchell, Ralph. *CQ's Guide to the U S. Constitution.* Washington, DC: Congressional Quarterly, Inc., 1986.

Peters, William. *A More Perfect Union: The Making of the United States Constitution.* New York: Crown Publishers, 1987.

Bibliography

Collier, Christopher, and James Lincoln Collier. *Decision in Philadelphia: The Constitutional Convention of 1787.* New York: Ballantine Books, 1986.

Kammen, Michael, ed. *The Origins of the American Constitution: A Documentary History.* New York: Penguin Books, 1986.

Mabie, Margot C. J. *The Constitution: Reflection of a Changing Nation.* New York: Henry Holt and Company, 1987.

Madison, James. *Notes of Debates in the Federal Convention of 1787, Bicentennial Edition.* New York: W. W. Norton & Co., 1987.

Source Notes

Introduction

1. William Peters, *A More Perfect Union: The Making of the United States Constitution*, (New York: Crown Publishers, 1987), p. 237.
2. Michael Kammen, ed., *The Origins of the American Constitution: A Documentary History* (New York: Penguin Books, 1986), p. 290.
3. Ibid., p. 288.

Chapter 1

1. William Peters, *A More Perfect Union: The Making of the United States Constitution* (New York: Crown Publishers, 1987), p. 279.
2. *Common Sense* by Thomas Paine, found at http://earlyamerica.com.
3. Article II, The Articles of Confederation.
4. Article III, The Articles of Confederation.
5. Edmund Lindop, *Birth of the Constitution* (Springfield, NJ: Enslow Publishers, 1987), p. 29.
6. Christopher Collier and James Lincoln Collier, *Decision in Philadelphia: The Constitutional Convention of 1787* (New York: Ballantine Books, 1986), p. 3.
7. Lindop, p. 40.
8. Collier and Collier, p. 34.
9. Richard Haesly, ed., *The Constitutional Convention* (San Diego: Greenhaven Press, 2002), pp. 82–83.

Chapter 2

1. Richard Haesly, *The Constitutional Convention* (San Diego: Greenhaven Press, 2002), p. 90.
2. "Vices of the Political System of the United States," at http://www.jmu.edu/madison/confweak.htm.
3. Ibid.
4. Ibid.
5. Michael Kammen, ed. *The Origins of the American Constitution: A Documentary History* (New York: Penguin Books, 1986), p. 22.
6. Christopher Collier and James Lincoln Collier, *Decision in Philadelphia: The Constitutional Convention of 1787* (New York: Ballantine Books, 1986) p. 60.
7. William Peters, *A More Perfect Union: The Making of the United States Constitution* (New York: Crown Publishers, 1987), page 2.
8. James Madison, *Notes of Debates in the Federal Convention of 1787* (New York: W.W. Norton & Co., 1987), page 31.

Chapter 3

1. James Madison, *Notes of Debates in the Federal Convention of 1787* (New York: W.W. Norton & Co., 1987), p. 30.
2. Ibid., p. 34.
3. Ibid., p. 34.
4. William Peters, *A More Perfect Union: The Making of the United States Constitution* (New York: Crown Publishers, 1987), pp. 39–40.
5. Madison, p. 35.
6. Ibid., p. 35.
7. Ibid., p. 97.
8. Edmund Lindop, *Birth of the Constitution* (Springfield, NJ: Enslow Publishers, 1987), p. 62.
9. Charles L. Mee, *The Genius of the People* (New York: Harper and Row, 1987), p. 169.

10. Madison, p. 142.
11. Peters, p. 94.
12. Richard Haesly, *The Constitutional Convention* (San Diego: Greenhaven Press, 2002), p. 82.
13. Catherine Drinker Bowen, *Miracle at Philadelphia* (Boston: Little, Brown and Company, 1966), p. 131.
14. Madison, p. 232.
15. Bowen, p. 140.
16. Madison, p. 224.
17. Ibid., p. 103.
18. Ibid., p. 411.
19. Ibid., p. 103.
20. Peters, p. 135.
21. Madison, p.e 390.
22. Ibid., p. 502.
23. Ibid., p. 506.

Chapter 4

1. William Peters, *A More Perfect Union: The Making of the United States Constitution*, (New York: Crown Publishers, 1987), p. 66.
2. James Madison, *Notes of Debates in the Federal Convention of 1787* (New York: W.W. Norton & Co., 1987), p. 39.
3. Ibid., p. 401.
4. Ibid., p. 404.
5. Peters, p. 17.
6. Madison, p. 172.
7. Edmund Lindop, *Birth of the Constitution* (Springfield, NJ: Enslow Publishers, 1987), p. 93.
8. Madison, p. 45.
9. Catherine Drinker Bowen, *Miracle at Philadelphia* (Boston: Little, Brown and Company, 1966), p. 60.
10. Madison, p. 46.
11. Ibid., p. 59.
12. Ibid., p.51.

13. Article II, Section I, the U.S. Constitution.
14. Madison, p. 606.
15. Ibid., p. 72.
16. Ibid., p. 67
17. Ibid., p. 67.
18. Charles L. Mee, *The Genius of the People* (New York: Harper and Row, 1987), p. 132.
19. Madison, p. 537.
20. Ibid., p. 537.
21. Article VI, the U.S. Constitution.

Chapter 5

1. James Madison, *Notes of Debates in the Federal Convention of 1787* (New York: W.W. Norton & Co., 1987), p. 630.
2. Ibid., p. 655.
3. Ibid., p. 654.
4. Ibid., p. 650.
5. Ibid., p. 613.
6. Ibid., p. 615.
7. Ibid., p. 566.
8. Ibid., p. 651.
9. Ibid., p. 659.
10. Edmund Lindop, *Birth of the Constitution* (Springfield, NJ: Enslow Publishers, 1987), p. 83.
11. Ibid., p. 87.

Primary Source Image List

Page 6: An early American woodcut entitled *The Blessings of the Constitution*.

Page 11: A picture of King John signing the Magna Carta in 1215.

Pages 12–13: *Bowles's New Pocket Map of the United States of America*, published in London in 1784, now housed in the Library of Congress.

Page 15: *The Stamp Act*, published in London in 1766, now housed in the Library of Congress.

Page 16: An engraving of King George III, created in 1802 by Robert Hartley, now in the Library of Congress.

Page 17: *The Boston Tea Party* by W. D. Cooper, engraved in 1789, now housed in the Library of Congress.

Page 19: At top, "Bloody Butchery of the British Troops," Salem, 1775, now housed in the Library of Congress. At bottom, *Thomas Paine*, an engraving by William Sharp, 1793, after a portrait by George Romney, now housed in the Library of Congress.

Page 22: Bottom right, *John Dickinson*, engraved by J. B. Forrest after a painting by Charles Wilson Peale. Above right, a portrait of Roger Sherman painted in 1902 by John Weir, after a miniature by John Trumbull.

Page 26: *Shays' Rebellion*, a woodcut from *Bickerstaff's Boston Almanack*, 1787.

Page 31: At top, *The Constitutional Convention*, 1787, engraved for *A History of the United States of America*, published by Huntington & Hopkins in 1823. Below left, a portrait of James Madison by Gilbert Stuart, now in the National Archives. Below right, a page from James Madison's notes taken at the Constitutional Convention, 1787, now with the Library of Congress.

Page 34: *The Works of John Locke*, Fourth Edition, London, 1740.

Page 36: The Assembly Room at Independence Hall, photograph courtesy of Independence National Historical Park.

Page 39: *The Constitutional Convention*, engraved in 1787.

Page 40: A portrait of Edmund Randolph by Constantino Brumidi, now in the rotunda of the United States Capitol building.

Page 42: *The Federal Edifice*, a cartoon in the *Massachusetts Centinel*, 1788.

Page 47: A portrait of Gouverneur Morris by Marchant.

Pages 50–51: An engraving possibly by Amos Doolittle, 1787, now in the Library of Congress.

Page 61: (Left to right, top to bottom)*George Mason*, etched by Albert Rosenthal in 1888. *Elbridge Gerry*, an oil painting by James Bogle, 1861. *Benjamin Franklin*, painted by Charles Wilson Peale in 1787. *Oliver Ellsworth*, painted by James Sharples. An engraving of John Rutledge after a painting by John Trumbull, now with the Library of Congress. An engraving of Abraham Baldwin, 1800.

Page 65: Watercolor by Benjamin Henry Latrobe, 1798, now with the Baltimore Historical Society.

Page 74: At left, *The Inauguration of George Washington*, 1789. At right, Washington's letter accepting the presidency.

Page 81: At left, a portrait of Chief Justice John Jay by Henry Peters Gray, from the collection of the United States Supreme Court. At right, the Old Royal Exchange Building, from a watercolor drawing owned by William Loring Andrews.

Page 91: Original draft of the U.S. Constitution, 1787, now housed at the Library of Congress.

Page 98: *Federal Hall*, a lithograph after an engraving by Cornelius Tiebout, now in the Library of Congress.

Index

About the Author

Heather Moehn is a freelance writer and editor in Boston, Massachusetts. Her nonfiction young adult books cover such diverse topics as world holidays, leukemia, and eating disorders. She has a B.A. in English from Carleton College.

Credits

Cover, p. 40, Architect of the Capitol; pp. 6, 15 (right), 39 © Bettmann/Corbis; pp. 11, 16 (bottom), 19 (bottom right), 22 (left), 61 (middle left, bottom left, bottom right), 74 © Hulton/Archive/Getty Images; pp. 12–13 Library of Congress Geography and Map Division; p. 15 (left) Library of Congress Manuscript Division; p. 16 (top) *The American Revolution: A Picture Source Book*, Dover Pictorial Archive Series; pp. 17, 19 (top) Library of Congress Rare Book and Special Collections Division; pp. 19 (bottom left), 22 (top right), 31 (top), 42, 50, 61 (top right), 90, 98 Library of Congress Prints and Photographs Division; p. 31(bottom left) National Archives and Records Administration Still Picture Branch; pp. 22 (bottom right), 47, 61(top left, middle right) Independence National Historical Park; p. 26 National Portrait Gallery, Smithsonian Institution/Art Resource, NY; p. 31 (bottom right) Library of Congress Madison Papers Manuscript Division; p. 34 © Archivo Iconografico, S.A./Corbis; p. 36, Lester Lefkowitz/Corbis; p. 65 The Maryland Historical Society, Baltimore, Maryland; p. 81 The Supreme Court of the United States Office of the Curator; p. 87 Record Group 11, General Records of the U.S. Government, Old Military and Civil Records, National Archives and Records Administration; p. 91 © Joseph Sohm, ChromoSohm Inc./Corbis.

Editor

Jake Goldberg

Design and Layout

Les Kanturek